Laura Payton

Shiba Inus

Everything About Selection, Care,
Nutrition, Behavior, and Training

BARRON'S

CONTENTS

SHIBA INU HISTORY

The Shiba Inu is one of six breeds in the same family of dogs native to Japan. Archaeological excavations, in northeast Japan, provided the discovery of bones from an ancient breed of dog existing in Japan between eight and ten thousand years ago.

Origin of the Shiba Inu

Recent advances in canine DNA studies provide evidence that domestic dogs are descendants of the Asian Gray Wolf. Several breeds, including the Shiba Inu, are classified as primitive, in that there have been few genetic alterations from the original wolf. One recent study analyzed the DNA from 85 recognized breeds of domesticated dogs. This study showed that the Shiba Inu has retained the DNA structure closest to the wolf of all of the breeds examined. The native breeds of Japan have stayed true to their origins, with minor changes over the years, resulting in a dog that is a study in contrasts: The Shiba is fiercely independent while loyal to his owner; The Shiba is reserved and dignified one moment and then frolicking like a puppy the next

Art and literature from the Edo period (approximately 300 years ago) provide a description of the native Japanese dog. The breed characteristics (described in detail in the following chapter) from these sources illustrate a dog with a prick ear with a slightly forward tilt, a double coat, a level back, moderate tuck up, and a high tail set. Illustrations show the dog with a ring, sickle, squirrel, or a gay tail. These same illustrations provide several clues to the original function of the breed. Most show the dog as a hunter, pursuing game ranging in size from bear, deer, and boar to small game, such as raccoon and rabbit, as well as varying types of fowl. Other illustrations show the dog as a guard dog, a watch dog, a fighting dog, and as a companion.

In 1928, Saito Hirokichi began the effort to protect and preserve the native Japanese breeds. In many regions the breeds were being mixed with other canine breeds, and the native Japanese dog was in danger of being lost. The

effort gained momentum and in 1932 the Japanese dog was designated a "national treasure." Shortly after this designation the organization Nihonken Hozonkai (Nippo) was formed to further these efforts.

The Shiba Inu, along with the other native Japanese breeds, faced extinction after World War II. Difficult economic conditions coupled with a widespread distemper epidemic dramatically reduced the native Japanese dog populations. The Nippo group actively began working with the local breeders to preserve these breeds, designated as National Treasures.

Breeds

The early efforts of Nippo focused on studying the art and literature to form a standard and a baseline of purity. Existing dogs were examined and carefully noted, paying particular attention to numbers and characteristics.

Nippo determined that the ancient Japanese dog had evolved into six breeds, largely due to regional isolation. These breeds have a baseline set of characteristics in common, with size and color or marking patterns providing the major distinction between the breeds. The Akita is classified as a large breed dog. The Shikoukou, the Kishu, the Hokaido, and the Kai are classified as midsize dogs, and the Shiba is categorized as a small breed of dog.

Of these six breeds existing in Japan today, five of the breeds are named after the region of Japan in which they evolved. Only the Shiba is not named for a particular region. The term *Shiba* had long been applied to the small dog by the residents of the Nagano area of Japan. No one knows precisely why the term Shiba was used to name these dogs. However, there are two common theories: Japanese is a kanji, or pictorially, based language. Many symbols have multiple meanings. The symbol for Shiba has

CHECKLIST

Non-Sporting Breeds

- ✔ American Eskimo Dog
- ✔ Bichon Frise
- ✔ Boston Terrier
- ✔ Bulldog
- ✔ Chinese Shar-Pei
- ✔ Chow Chow
- ✔ Dalmatian
- ✔ Finnish Spitz
- ✔ French Bulldog
- ✔ Keeshond
- ✔ Lhasa Apso
- ✔ Löwchen
- ✔ Norwegian Lundehund
- ✔ Poodle (Miniature)
- ✔ Poodle (Standard)
- ✔ Schipperke
- ✔ Shiba Inu
- ✔ Tibetan Spaniel
- ✔ Tibetan Terrier
- ✔ Xoloitzcuintli

multiple meanings, as well. One meaning is for a type of shrub frequently translated as brushwood. Some feel the dog was named for the bush or shrub, to reflect the hunting heritage. Shibas are tenacious hunters, entering dense foliage in pursuit of game. Another meaning of the word Shiba is to wither or wilt. Still another theory purports that the Shiba was named for its predominant color, red. The foliage in the Nagano region of Japan in the fall when the leaves are turning is a vivid orange, very similar to the correct red in the Shiba coat.

The term *inu* or *ken* simply means "dog" in Japanese. The official name of the breed as designated by the American Kennel Club (AKC) is the Shiba Inu. Throughout much of the world the Shiba Inu is alternately called the Shiba Ken. You may notice breeders and owners familiar with the breed chuckle when people refer to the Shiba Inu dog. This is because they are in essence saying "the Shiba dog dog."

Temperament: Kan-i, Ryosei, and Soboku

Kan-i

The Japanese have three words often used to define the essence of the Shiba: *kan-i, ryosei,* and *soboku. Kan-i* is defined as a boldness of spirit combined with alertness and a keen sense of awareness. Kan-i embodies the confidence of a dog that knows her own worth. The Shiba is aware of her surroundings at all times. This sense of awareness allows the Shiba to recognize friend from foe. The Shiba will not shy away from a threat nor will she react with unwarranted aggression. A confident Shiba stands her ground willing to defend herself and her family if the need arises. Many Shiba owners state their Shiba won't start a fight, but will be happy to finish one.

At the entrance or gates of many temples or plazas in Japan, stand statues on either side serving as guardians. These guardians are stylized statues resembling many types of animals, both real and mythical. It is stated that if you understand the purpose and intent of the guardians, you will understand kan-i. The guardian is always watchful, alert, and prepared to guard his domain with every fiber of his being, but at rest, calmly and patiently observing until the need arises. The Shiba should always display kan-i—calm and alert unless a threat is detected, at which time the Shiba responds in a manner that matches the specific threat.

Ryosei

Good-natured is the literal meaning of the term *ryosei*. The Shiba should be obedient, faithful, loyal, and under the control of her owner to have good nature. The Shiba is respectful of her owner and obeys commands when given, while being true to her own nature.

Soboku

Country-girl beauty is the literal meaning of the term *soboku*. The Shiba is beautiful in a manner that is natural, not contrived or artificial. She has a beauty that is simple, yet elegant, unsophisticated, yet poised. The Shiba is the "girl next door" of the dog world. She is always present, loyal, and faithful with a natural beauty; she does not push herself forward with a beauty that is cosmetic or artificial. "What you see is what you get" typifies the Shiba and the term soboku.

Popularity Worldwide

Today the Shiba is enjoying popularity around the globe. This "Japanese treasure" has been discovered outside of Japan and its popularity is growing rapidly. Today, the Shiba is actively bred, exhibited, and a significant addition to families as a companion pet in many parts of Asia, North America, Europe, Australia, and South America.

The first Shibas to come to the United States arrived in the 1950s as companion pets to servicemen returning home from tours in Japan. The American Shiba population continued to grow and by the early 1990s several significant and influential breeding programs had been established in the United States. At this point in breed history, the process of obtaining AKC acceptance began.

The Non-Sporting Group

The Shiba Inu was recognized by the AKC as a member of the Non-Sporting Group in June of 1993. Many fanciers of the Shiba were disappointed by AKC's inclusion of the Shiba into the Non-Sporting Group as this natural

hunter has more in common with the dogs in the Sporting, Working, or even Terrier Groups, than those in the Non-Sporting Group. The Shiba with soboku, "country girl beauty," to be shown in a natural state seems to have little in common with her grooming-intensive sisters in the Non-Sporting Group.

During the last few years, the AKC has considered realigning the groups to cluster the breeds with others that share function, characteristics, and type traits. The most recent attempt was not approved. However, it is important to note that in each realignment proposal presented, the Shiba Inu has been removed from the Non-Sporting Group. It is likely that the next proposal, if requested and approved, will place the Shiba Inu in a group more closely aligned with the function and traits of comparable breeds.

PHYSICAL CHARACTERISTICS OF THE SHIBA INU

What are the characteristics that define any breed? Most breeders will tell you it is a combination of three factors: type, structure, and temperament.

The Shiba is a visually striking dog. Shiba owners will tell you that wherever they go with their Shiba, strangers both human and canine will approach for a visit. When strolling along with a Shiba it is not uncommon to be approached with questions such as, "What is that?" If the Shiba is red in color the first question is, "Is that a fox?" If your Shiba companion's color is red sesame the approach is usually, "Is that a coyote?" The black and tan elicits the query "Is that a wolf?" No matter the color, you will be greeted with a variety of questions. After a variety of questions, you will occasionally encounter someone that recognizes the breed type and will startle you with the question, "Is that a Shiba Inu"?

Type refers to the traits or physical characteristics that make a breed unique, distinguishing one breed from another, such as color, markings, eye shape, ear placement, carriage, etc. Structure refers to skeletal and muscular features of the breed developed so the individual dog can perform the functions he was bred to accomplish. Temperament refers to the traits of "personality" that distinguish the breed and again work hand in hand with the elements of type and structure allowing the individual dog to perform her job.

Type Characteristics

The traits that define Shiba type comprise several areas: coloration, marking patterns, tail set, coat texture, and the features of the head, comprising eye shape, ears, skull shape, muzzle, and dentition.

Color

One of the most striking characteristics of the Shiba is the vivid color. The Shiba has three typical colors: red, red sesame, and black and tan. These colors represent the color of the coat covering the main portion of the dog's body. In addition to the colored portion of the coat, all Shibas should have urajiro, or a pattern of white or cream colored coat hair.

Urajiro appears on the cheeks, the sides of the muzzle, the underside of the muzzle, the neck, the chest, belly, underside of the tail, and the inside of the dogs legs. The fourth color that appears in the Shiba Inu is cream or white.

Red: Red is the genetically dominant and most common color in the Shiba Inu. While the red can vary from a pale orange to almost a buff color, to a deep mahogany red, the ideal color is a vivid orange. It is the vivid orange when contrasted with the typical urajiro, or marking pattern, that give the Shiba her fox-like appearance. Most foxes in nature do not actually display this color, however, the stylized or cartoon caricature of the fox will typically show similar color patterning as the Shiba.

Black with Tan Points: The black and tan Shiba is often referred to as a tri-colored dog by exhibitors and judges of other breeds. Shiba fanciers understand that uragiro is a required component of the coat pattern for Shibas of all colors, and is understood to be a feature of type. Therefore, it is not designated in the definitions of color. Reds are not called red and whites, and black and tans are not referred to as tri-colored. The black coat is not a blue black color and is usually not a solid black color. The guard coat, as it separates and stands off from the body, allows the observer a glimpse of the undercoat, breaking the image of a solid black color. When the black and tan Shiba has lost her undercoat, she will, for a short period, have a more solid black appearance to her coat.

While the borders between black, tan, and white are defined and not muddy, the colors should blend gradually and not appear penciled or painted. Tan points are typically found as two oval spots over the eyes, on the sides of the muzzle between the black bridge of the muzzle and the white cheeks, on the outside of the legs, on the feet, and occasionally on the inside of the ear and on the underside of the tail.

Red Sesame: The red sesame is a red Shiba with black tipped hairs that are interspersed evenly with the red colored guard coat. The key element is that the black is interspersed evenly and is not patterned or in solid patches. The amount of black distributed evenly through the coat may be light or very heavy. This color pattern is considered by many breeders to be the most difficult color to breed correctly. Many Shibas designated as red sesame are in reality red Shibas with black hair inserts. Due to the difficulty of breeding the red sesame with the correct color pattern, few breeders focus on the sesame or plan a breeding to produce the red sesame color. Most breeders, when color is the main consideration, plan a breeding to produce either reds or black and tans. The correctly colored red sesame Shiba is a beautiful dog, however they are few and far between.

In simple terms, the red is the dominant color of the Shiba. The black and tan is the recessive color. The red sesame is the product of the combination of the red and black genes. Shiba breeders have coined several terms to clarify color genetics. While the terms are generally understood among breeders, these terms often are confusing for those not deeply entrenched in the fancy.

While a Shiba may be red in color, this Shiba may have one red parent and one black parent. Because this Shiba carries the red gene and the black gene, even though he is red, he is often referred to as a "genetic sesame" or a red sesame for breeding purposes. The red sesame or the genetic sesame may pass either the red or the black gene to his offspring. A "clear red" is a Shiba that only carries the red gene and will only pass the red gene to his offspring. A series of tables is given in Appendix E providing the color inheritance patterns for the Shiba.

Color inheritance in the Shiba is thought to be a product of two gene pairs: one for color and one for a dilution factor. If the dilution factor is present in both parents and if the factor is passed to a puppy from both parents, then the cream color is produced.

Cream: The cream color is a serious fault in the show ring. However, this cosmetic characteristic has no bearing on the suitability of a cream Shiba as a companion. There is no known adverse health issues associated with this color pattern.

There is a controversy surrounding faulting of the cream color in the show ring. Some feel that since the color occurs naturally in the breed, then the color should not be faulted in the ring. In Japan, the color is faulted, so in keeping with the country of origin, the AKC Standard faults the cream as well.

There are two main reasons why the cream is faulted. The Shiba must display a distinct urajiro pattern to be correct. The cream color does not allow for this marking pattern to be distinct. Additionally, in Japan, the cream or white color is associated with the Kishu breed. It is theorized the cream color (or dilution factor) became a trait in the Shiba through cross-breeding with the Kishu, in times past. A concentrated effort has been made, both in Japan and the other countries who have adopted the Shiba, to eliminate the color or dilution factor from the gene pools.

Markings

There is a distinction between urajiro and markings. As stated previously, urajiro is a feature of the Shiba that is present in all of the three preferred colors, with placement on the body defined to specific areas. Any extra white patterning is referred to as markings. The typical red Shiba is designated as red on the registration papers. If the same red Shiba were to have a white tail tip, white

tion of these four carriage patterns. The tail should be set relatively high on the body where the Shiba's rear legs extend beyond the body outline and the tail.

The tail is frequently a barometer of mood in the Shiba. When a Shiba is fearful, tense, or uneasy the tail may drop. While several tail sets are acceptable, the tail itself should not drop. This feature of type becomes an indicator of temperament. The bold and spirited Shiba carries his tail erect. A shiba may drop his tail when he hears a loud noise, and moments later when he knows all is well, carry his tail up again.

socks, or any other white marking not defined as urajiro, the registration papers should list the dog as red with white markings. The same situation is applied to the red sesame and the black and tan. Typical marking patterns include a solid patch on the tip of the tail, a collar extending the chest markings around the neck, white markings on the legs that extend beyond the elbow, and solid white or cream patches on the body. Conversely, the pinto marking pattern occurs when a large portion of the body is white or cream and the colored guard coat appears in marking patterns that are similar to traditional urajiro placement or other marking patterns.

Tail Set

The Shiba's tail should have thick hair that resembles a bottle brush. The carriage of the tail varies from Shiba to Shiba. The two carriage patterns most frequently observed are the "makio" or a loose single curl and the "sashio" where the tail tip does not cross the back, riding parallel to back as the dog moves. Other variations include a tail with a double curl; a "sickle" tail, where the tail is carried upright perpendicular to the body; or a varia-

Coat Texture

The guard coat on the Shiba should be stiff and prickly and placed evenly on the body. The correct guard coat is not plush or soft—it should almost hurt to touch. Having said this, the correct Shiba coat is rare. Breeders are actively working to improve the texture of the coat, as well as having an even placement of guard hair on the body. Occasionally, a long coat Shiba is produced. This Shiba has a coat that is quite a bit longer and gives the Shiba a fluffy appearance. This is faulted in the show ring, but as with the cream color, this is a cosmetic fault and there are no known heath factors or problems associated with this coat.

Head

The Shiba's head is quite distinctive—many of the features that typify the Shiba are found on the head. Perhaps the first thing one will notice when looking at the Shiba is her facial expression. The Shiba is alert and confident.

She may appear curious and inquisitive or simply aware of everything going on around her. Even if your Shiba does not seem to be paying attention, make no mistake, she is aware of her environment.

Eyes

The head of the Shiba consists of a series of lines or planes. The correct placement of the eye is no exception. If you draw an imaginary line beginning at the inner corner of the eye (corner closest to the muzzle) through the outer corner of the eye and extend the line to the edge of the skull, the line should run to the base of the ear. The shape of the eye is somewhat triangular. The lower rim of the eye is slightly rounded and the upper lid gathers in a slightly triangular shape. The Shiba's eyes are a deep brown, although occasionally the color can range from an amber color to a lighter brown.

Ear Set

The ears of the Shiba are another barometer of her mood. When greeting a friend, she may pin her ears back in an expression that closely resembles a smile. While walking through a neighborhood, her ears may be in constant motion as she listens to her environment. The Shiba's ears are similar to the eye in that the shape is somewhat triangular. The correct ear will curve slightly along the outer edge and be closer to a straight line along the inner edge. Occasionally, a Shiba will have a reverse ear set, where the inner edge is curved and the outer edge is straight. The reverse ear is not desirable in a show dog, however it is a cosmetic trait that will cause no known problems for a companion pet.

The ears are in proportion to the rest of the head and are not positioned too close together or too far apart. The ear is not upright and does not fold. The ears pitch forward slightly and form a slight cup as they tilt forward. The fur on the outer ear is the color of the body, while the fur on the inner ear is typically lighter in color ranging from a light red or tan to a cream or white color.

Muzzle

The Shiba's muzzle appears somewhat circular in shape when viewed from the front due to the full lower jaw. The lower muzzle should not be flat or narrow. The muzzle is slightly narrower at the tip than at the cheeks. The lips are tight and firm and are black in color,

breeds that are unfamiliar with the Shiba notice the Shiba's bite immediately. These individuals are surprised that such a small dog has such big teeth. The Shiba's mouth is more suited to tearing or ripping than a bird dog's mouth, which is designed to retrieve and return the game. Remember, the Shiba is a hunter! She was bred to hunt boar and the powerful jaw with large teeth illustrate this heritage better than any of her other features.

Structural Characteristics

The bones and joints of the Shiba should align to allow her to move easily through many types of terrain. It is important to understand your Shiba's structure before you attempt certain physical activities. The typical Shiba will gamely attempt any physical activity asked of her, whether or not she is structurally suited to the task. It is a good idea to speak with your veterinarian about the activities you plan to engage in with your Shiba. If your Shiba has physical or structural limitations, the importance of understanding any restrictions will help to prevent debilitating injuries. The traits that define Shiba structure comprise several areas: height, weight, proportion, substance, musculature, and body outline.

Height, Proportion, Weight, and Substance

The proportion of the body is roughly 10:11, with the length of the back (11 parts) slightly longer than the height at the shoulder (10 parts). The ideal height range for males is 14.5" to 16.5" (36.8 cm to 41.9 cm) and 13.5" to 15.5" (34.3 cm to 39.4 cm) for the females. The measurement is from the ground to the

as is the nose. The line of the muzzle from the cheek to the nose is straight. The muzzle is in proportion to the head.

Head Shape

The overall head is in proportion to the body and is one of the distinctive features of the Shiba. The forehead is broad and flat and extends upward to the top of the skull. The portion of the skull between the ears is very slightly rounded. The forehead may have a small indentation or furrow. The head is distinct without being exaggerated.

Dentition

The Shiba has a full compliment of powerful teeth. Many individuals familiar with other withers. There is still a large variance in height for this mid-sized breed with many Shibas below or above the desirable range. This size gap is narrowing as breeders focus on stabilizing the size within the middle of the range.

Most male Shibas range in weight from 22 to 28 pounds (10 kg to 13 kg) and the females are typically between 15 to 19 pounds (7 kg to 9 kg). The weight should match the size of the body. Taller male Shibas may weigh more than 28 pounds (13 kg) and shorter females weigh less than 15 pounds (7 kg). Care should be taken to avoid weight extremes in either direction. If your Shiba's weight appears too high or too low, consult with your veterinarian for options to bring the weight within the desirable range.

The bone structure of the Shiba is in balance with her body frame. The bones are not thick and the Shiba is not considered to be a big-boned dog. The bones are not thin or spindly, giving the Shiba an appearance of fragility. The bone density for the Shiba is moderate, allowing her to make quick adjustments in direction and to cover ground quickly and effortlessly for extended periods of time.

Musculature and Body Carriage

The body of the Shiba is compact and well muscled. She does not have overly developed muscles that will restrict or interfere with her move-ment, nor are her muscles weak, inhibiting her ability to move as required. The Shiba should give the appearance of an endurance athlete—well conditioned and able to travel over various types of terrain without tiring. She is alert and displays curiosity and an awareness of her surroundings.

The function of the Shiba is to hunt. The typical Shiba combines all of her senses for hunting. While moving freely, without the restraint of a leash, the Shiba will carry her head forward in line with her back or slightly lowered to pick up scent along the ground. She is alert to the sounds in her environment with hearing that is very sensitive. She is however, frequently a visual hunter. She may stand posed like a statue with only her eyes moving to lure game into the open area. Even while in motion she is visually scanning her environment, alert to any slight movement. She will carry herself with confidence and an awareness of her place in the world—at the top. The bold Shiba enters any new environment and says "I am here and I am ready to meet any new challenge."

Body Outline: The back of the Shiba is straight and firm from the base of the neck to the base of the tail. The body from the front of the chest to the firmly tucked up waist is an egg-shaped oval. The oval is wider at the chest and narrower at the loin or waist—the portion of the body containing the lumbar vertebrae before the pelvic crest and behind the rib cage. The depth of chest meets or is slightly above the elbow. The spring or curve of the ribs is moderate with the correct ratio

CHECKLIST

Physical Characteristics

✔ Prick Ear—The ear is carried erect. The shape is usually triangular with a point at the tip.

✔ Level Back—The outline from the point behind the withers and tail set is level or straight.

✔ Moderate Tuck Up—Displaying a shallower body depth at the loin than is displayed at the chest.

✔ High Tail Set—The base of the tail sets high on the rump.

✔ Ring Tail Set—The tail is carried up and curves around almost completing a ring or circle.

✔ Sickle Tail Set—The tail is carried out and up in a semicircle over the back.

✔ Squirrel Tail Set—The tail is carried up and is carried forward running more or less parallel to the back, without completing a ring.

✔ Gay Tail Set—The tail is carried upright and is carried almost perpendicular to the back.

✔ Withers—Located just behind the neck, and marked by the highest point of the shoulder.

✔ Muzzle—The portion of the head in front of the eyes; includes nasal bone, jaws, and nostrils.

✔ Dewclaw—The fifth toe on the front feet. The dewclaw is an extra and unused appendage.

✔ Loin—Located along the back, it is the region between the last ribs and the hindquarters.

✔ Hock—The dog's heel comprised of the bones of the hind leg that form the joint between the metatarsus and the second thigh.

✔ Pastern—The portion of the foreleg between the wrist and the toes.

✔ Occiput—The upper back point of the skull.

✔ Overshot—The front incisors overlap leaving a gap between the teeth of the upper and lower jaw when the mouth is closed.

✔ Undershot—The incisors of the lower jaw project beyond the front teeth of the upper jaw when the mouth is closed.

of bone to cartilage to provide the lung capacity required for endurance. The prosternum or breastbone of the Shiba is not exaggerated, nor is it absent. Shibas with too little prosternum are often referred to as chicken or pigeon breasted when the breastbone is buried in fat or muscle. An exaggerated or absent prosternum places the Shiba at risk for injury due to improper attachment of the muscles or ligaments required for movement. The tail is set high at the base of the loin and balances the rest of the body. The strong and powerful neck

ascends from the withers in an arch that continues to the tip of the ears.

Forequarters: There are several bones that work in harmony to create the Shiba's front end assembly. It is the bones and joints of this assembly that create the reaching action for forward movement. The shoulder blade, the humerus, the radius, the ulna, the carpus, the metacarpus, and the joints associated with these bones, form the composition and foundation of the Shiba's front end, which is designed for ease of motion.

The angle created by the joining of the humerus and the shoulder blade is the basis for determining the front end angulation of an individual dog or breed. The degree of this angle or hinge point is determined by the location where the upper portion of the shoulder blade approaches the thoracic vertebrae and the lower end of the humerus joins the radius creating the elbow joint. Some dogs are designed with more open angles or a wider distance between the withers and the elbow, the line that creates the base of the triangle with the vertex of the triangle, the junction of the humerus, and shoulder blade. This open shoulder is usually accompanied by a curving croup or roached back to create the balance required for ease of motion. The Shiba, like most working breeds, moves more fluidly with a 45 degree angle in the front end assembly with the shoulder blade and upper arm (humerus) close to equal in length.

In some Shibas the shoulders are too straight or the angulation resembles the more

Male Height Chart

Standard	Ideal	Minimum	Maximum	Point of Measurement
Nippo	15.55 inches (39.5 cm)	14.96 inches (38 cm)	16.14 inches (41 cm)	behind the withers
JKC	15.75 inches (40 cm)	15.16 inches (38.5 cm)	16.34 inches (41.5 cm)	at the withers
AKC	15.50 inches (39.3 cm)	14.50 inches (36.8 cm)	16.50 inches (41.9 cm)	at the withers

Female Height Chart

Standard	Ideal	Minimum	Maximum	Point of Measurement
Nippo	14.37 inches (36.5 cm)	13.78 inches (35 cm)	14.96 inches (38 cm)	behind the withers
JKC	14.57 inches (37 cm)	13.98 inches (35.5 cm)	15.16 inches (38.5 cm)	at the withers
AKC	14.50 inches (36.8 cm)	13.50 inches (34.3 cm)	15.50 inches (39.3 cm)	at the withers

open shoulder angles described previously. The straight shoulder creates several difficulties for the dog in motion and can place the Shiba at risk for injury and joint degeneration. When the shoulders are too wide or too tight, the Shiba will not move as effortlessly as she should. This can result in long term joint issues or straining her muscles or tendons.

The Shiba legs are straight and parallel to each other. The spacing between the legs is balanced with the placement of the elbow, which is set tightly against the rib cage. The feet of the Shiba are slightly rounded and shaped like those of a cat. The pads on the bottom of the feet are thick to protect the Shiba in varying climates and a broad spectrum of terrain.

Hindquarters: One of the most frequent health issues diagnosed in the Shiba Inu is patellar luxation. This occurs with increasing frequency due to structural deficiencies in the dog's rear end assembly. The driving force for canine movement is the hindquarters of the dog. The angles of the hindquarters should be in balance with those of the front. This balance allows the front and rear of the dog to work in harmony. Structural misalignment will result in the Shiba shifting the distribution of where she carries the weight of her body. When the rear is not aligned properly, the weight-bearing distribution shifts and stresses other parts of the body in a manner that makes the Shiba prone to injury or deterioration in the joints. It is not uncommon to see weakness in the rear legs in geriatric Shibas. For this reason, it is important to understand any structural weakness in your Shiba before undertaking certain physical activities. The typical Shiba will engage in various physical activities from running to jumping to leaping. Make an effort to encourage activities that complement her inherent physical capabilities.

Temperament

The Shiba is a bold and confident dog. The typical Shiba does not understand that she is not the biggest dog in the park and will frequently initiate eye contact with dogs that are significantly larger than she is. This type of dominance characteristic can place the Shiba in a difficult position with other dogs. In areas where dogs are unrestrained, such as a dog park, it is important that Shiba owners closely monitor interaction with other dogs. Certain breeds, such as the Great Pyrenees were bred to emphasize traits that make them excellent flock guardians. These dogs inherently understand that a wolf is a threat to a flock of sheep. With the Shiba's similarity to the wolf, some breeds may view your Shiba as a threat. The confident attitude of the Shiba is not helpful in this type of a situation. It is important for the safety of both dogs that the owners limit behaviors that can quickly escalate into confrontation. The typical Shiba may not start the argument, but will not hesitate to finish it, once engaged.

Shibas should not be aggressive with people, and are usually willing to interact with anyone that is willing to play with them. Some may be indifferent with strangers and are slow to warm up to people that are unfamiliar. A word of caution is in order with small children or older children that may behave aggressively with dogs. Some Shibas are very patient and are willing to put up with quite a bit and will withdraw when the child's actions make them uncomfortable. There are some that have a lower threshold for nonsense—ear and

tail pulling may result in a snap at a child. Shibas should be socialized with children from a young age and common sense on the part of the owner will prevent many difficult situations. When a Shiba withdraws from company, it is never a good idea to force her to engage. A simpler approach is to provide your guest with a toy or a treat and manage introductions and ongoing interaction in a manner that is comfortable for both your Shiba and your guest.

The Standards

The Shiba is classified as a small dog in Japan (the country of origin). However, in the United States, it is more frequently referred to as a small- to mid-size dog. There are three primary standards that define the ideal Shiba for conformation judging in the dog show arena: The Nippo Standard, the Federation Cynologique Internationale (FCI) Standard and the American Kennel Club (AKC) Standard. Nippo has one standard for the six native Japanese breeds with judging sheets or notes to define the distinctions between the breeds. The FCI Standard is the universal standard, based on the standard of the country of origin, in the case of the Shiba, Japan Kennel Club or JKC. At most dog shows held in the United States, the AKC Standard is the benchmark for judging the Shiba. A copy of the complete AKC Shiba Inu Standard is presented in Appendix C. The three standards are similar in many regards and the main points will be outlined below. There are a few areas that differ among the different standards, and those are in the areas of dentition and height.

The AKC Standard differs from the other two prevailing standards with regard to denti-

Terms Defined

Prick Ear: The ear is carried erect. The shape is usually triangular with a point at the tip.

Level Back: The outline from the point behind the withers and tail set is level or straight.

Moderate Tuck Up: Displaying a shallower body depth at the loin than is displayed at the chest.

High Tail Set: The base of the tail sets high on the rump.

Ring Tail Set: The tail is carried up and curves around almost completing a ring or circle.

Sickle Tail Set: The tail is carried out and up in a semicircle over the back.

Squirrel Tail Set: The tail is carried up and is carried forward running more or less parallel to the back, without completing a ring.

Gay Tail Set: The tail is carried upright and is carried almost perpendicular to the back.

Withers: Located just behind the neck, and marked by the highest point of the shoulder.

Muzzle: The portion of the head in front of the eyes; includes nasal bone, jaws, and nostrils.

Dewclaw: The fifth toe on the front feet. The dewclaw is an extra and unused appendage.

Loin: Located along the back, it is the region between the last ribs and the hindquarters.

Hock: The dog's heel comprised of the bones of the hind leg which form the joint between the metatarsus and the second thigh.

Pastern: The portion of the foreleg between the wrist and the toes.

Occiput: The upper back point of the skull.

Overshot: The front incisors overlap leaving a gap between the teeth of the upper and lower jaw when the mouth is closed.

Undershot: The incisors of the lower jaw project beyond the front teeth of the upper jaw when the mouth is closed.

---

tion. Both the Nippo and FCI seriously fault any missing teeth. Some of the first Shibas imported into the United States had missing teeth. As a result, some breeding programs have had difficulty producing full dentition in the puppies. Breeders throughout the United States are actively striving for full dentition in their breeding programs. It is likely that in the future, the U.S. Standard may change to fault three or more missing teeth or to fault any missing teeth, depending upon how soon members of the NSCA agree to a change.

The range allowance for height is one of the principal areas of controversy in the Shiba around the world. The AKC Standard is the only standard that allows an overlap in the size of males and females. The Nippo Standard provides for the measurement on the back, behind the withers. The ideal measurement at this point is 15.55 inches (39.5 cm) for males and 14.37 inches (36.5 cm) for females. A variance of 1.5 cm is allowed in either direction. The FCI Standard provides for the measurement at the withers. The ideal measurement is 15.75 inches (40 cm) for males and 14.37 inches (37 cm) for females. A variance of 1.5 cm is allowed in either direction.

See the table on page 20 containing a summary of the allowable height ranges in the three standards.

CONSIDERATIONS BEFORE YOU BUY

The Shiba has inherited the traits of the ancient Japanese dog. With a fiercely independent nature and the powerful jaws and body of an intense hunter, the Shiba does not bend her will easily.

Is the Shiba the Right Dog for You?

The Shiba is extremely intelligent and is a problem-solving breed. She is a great observer and will watch patterns and routines to determine the best way to accomplish her desires. Shibas are well-known escape artists: She will figure out how to open gates, break out of crates, slip from a leash, and escape through doorways.

The Shiba will also determine the weakest link in the household discipline chain. If all but one member of the household will not feed her from the table, the Shiba quickly learns to position herself by the family member who will slip her treats during the family's mealtime. The Shiba requires consistency above all else during the training process. Raising a Shiba is like raising a child. If you tell a child his bed-time is 8:00 P.M., the first time he stays up until 8:30 P.M., the bedtime is never 8:00 P.M. again. If you have the ability to consistently apply discipline, even when a cute, cuddly fur ball is licking your face immediately after shredding every plant in the living room, then you may have what it takes to raise a feisty Shiba puppy into a well-behaved adult.

The Commitment

The average life span of the Shiba is 14 years. Sharing your life with a Shiba can provide you many years of companionship with a loving and loyal "best friend" whose intelligence and intuitive nature will never cease to amaze you. However, to get to this stage, you will need to spend the first year socializing and training with consistency and vigilance. Dog ownership is a serious commitment, regardless

of the breed selected. The financial investment, consisting of the initial cost of the dog, veterinary care, and feeding and caring for the dog is only one aspect of your commitment. More significant is the time commitment you are making with the addition of your new family member.

Timing Considerations

Selecting the right time to bring your new family member into your home is as important as selecting the right individual of the right breed. Work with your breeder to determine when a puppy will be available to you, as well as the right time of the year, taking into consideration the existing demands on your time. The first few months will require more frequent exercise periods to assist in the housebreaking process, and as such will place more demands on your time. During the first six months some form of obedience training is suggested. Find out when obedience training programs in your area are offered, and schedule your new arrival accordingly.

Many breeders receive a plethora of calls around the holiday season from individuals inquiring about puppies. While a breeder may have puppies available in this time frame, you may find the breeder reluctant to place a puppy at this time. There are several reasons for this. Three of the main reasons are:

1. It is never a good idea to select a puppy as a gift for another person. That person may not desire a dog or have the time or financial resources to honor the commitment you have made for him or her.

2. The holiday season is generally a busy time for most families. Travel and time commitments are not compatible with the time

---

═══ T I P ═══

Compatibility Quiz
✔ Do you enjoy a dog that does not particularly need you?
✔ Do you enjoy a dog that is content to spend time alone?
✔ Do you mind if a dog ignores you when she chooses?
✔ Do you enjoy a dog that will participate in a wide variety of physical activities?
✔ Do you enjoy a dog that is playful or mischievous in nature?
✔ Are you comfortable taking a vigilant role to assure that your dog does not run loose?
✔ Do you enjoy a dog that is loyal and protective?
✔ Are you patient and content to work hard to train your dog?
✔ Will you have difficulty being consistent with discipline and training?
✔ Do you enjoy a dog with minimal grooming requirements?
✔ Will you be bothered by a dog that routinely sheds her coat?
✔ Are you prepared to train your dog to eliminate dog aggression, and if that doesn't work, to keep your dog from aggressive contact with other dogs?

---

requirements involved in adding a new puppy to the family.

3. The holiday season is often a season of loneliness or emotional stress. While a new puppy may seem like a good choice for filling an emotional void, in a few months, after the stress of the season has faded, the puppy may prove to be an additional source of stress, instead of providing the comfort desired. It is better to think your decision through and make the decision to add a new puppy logically, without relying only on emotion or sentimentality.

Another common pitfall to avoid is to add a new puppy to your household shortly after losing another pet. One pet can never truly replace another. Be sure to allow time for the grieving process before adopting a new puppy. Many dedicated dog lovers cannot imagine living without a dog, and find the emptiness of living without one difficult. Please take time to consider if the time is right for you to add a pet without placing unfair expectations on a young puppy.

Potential Drawbacks to the Shiba Inu

The Shiba is seldom an off-lead breed; the Shiba is an instinctive hunter and will react to anything moving as prey. A squirrel, rabbit, bird, cat, or plastic bag blowing in the wind becomes the object of their attention and they will tear off after their prey. When the Shiba is on the hunt, she is extremely focused. She tunes out everyone and everything else. She will not hear you call, scream, beg, grovel, plead, or cry. Many Shibas have met a premature end because they ran in front of a car while hunting their prey.

Dog Aggression

The Shiba was bred to be an independent thinker and an independent hunter. Occasion-

ally, the hunters used them in male/female pairs, but more often they were bred and taught to work with their owner and not other dogs. Additionally, part of the history of the Japanese breeds involves the use of these dogs in dog fighting. While dog fighting was traditionally reserved for the larger members of the Japanese family of dogs, the smaller Shiba still maintains the agility, tenacity, and ferocity of her larger cousins. The "never say die" spirit of these breeds is such that once committed to a dog fight, they may not back down until they are physically unable to continue fighting.

Fortunately, the sport of fighting dogs is illegal in most jurisdictions in the United States. The popularity of this sport has faded worldwide and dog aggression is not a desired trait in most breeds. However, these traits have been selectively bred into the breed and it will take time to breed away from these tendencies. Many breeders cite temperament as the top priority in a breeding program. Vigilant training may help to overcome this instinctual trait. Early socialization with other dogs is one way to help train out these behaviors, as well as spaying or neutering your Shiba at a relatively young age. However, some Shibas will have this tendency more strongly than others, and you may never be able to train out this trait. You may find yourself crossing the street when you see another dog approaching to avoid conflict.

Coat Shed

The Shiba has a double coat. This coat is genetically designed to help your dog survive in harsh climates and a variety of weather conditions. The Shiba has two different types of fur. One is a harsh outer coat, consisting of guard hair. The dog's predominant color comes from this coat. It is stiff and stands off from the body. The guard coat is designed to repel water, protecting the Shiba from the elements. The second coat is the softer and dense undercoat. This coat is most often cream, white, buff, or grayish in color and serves as insulation.

A typical Shiba will shed her undercoat twice per year. The Shiba does not shed continuously as some breeds will, but when she does, it is significant. You will find Shiba fur balls everywhere. An unprepared first-time Shiba owner may think something is very wrong with her Shiba when facing the first coat shed. You may find yourself amazed that your little dog had that much coat in the first place when you are picking the fur up from the floor. Rigorous brushing will minimize the amount of fur you will find around your house and some vitamin treatments claim to reduce the coat shed, but nothing eliminates the coat shedding process completely.

Training

Your Shiba is a very unique animal and will most likely think her way is the better option, instead of following your directions when you begin the training process. She is a problem solver and will work diligently to show you the better way. She may not respond to many typical training methods. Some dogs will look at you and seem to say, "What can I do for you?" while the Shiba looks at you and seems to be saying, "What's in it for me?" or "Why should I do that?" Often food or toys will provide the stimulation required for training. A simple voice command, frequently repeated, may not gain the Shiba's attention.

The Shiba is often the class clown of any obedience course. While the other dogs are sitting and staying as instructed, your Shiba may decide that is the time to wander the room, look for treats dropped on the floor, or visit the dogs at the end of the line. Your Shiba may decide at this point she has had enough, and head for the door because she is ready to go home. Patience on your part and that of your instructor is definitely required.

Strengths of the Shiba Inu

The Shiba has many positive traits that make her a desirable companion. Balance the drawbacks and strengths of the breed to determine if a Shiba is compatible with your personality and lifestyle.

Cleanliness

The typical Shiba is very clean and is almost born housetrained. You may observe the Shiba grooming herself, like a cat. Shibas are often meticulous and refuse to soil their area. Some Shibas don't like the rain and will look at you as if you have lost your mind when offering them exercise during a storm. These Shibas look at you and seem to say, "I'm staying here where it's dry; let's wait until the rain stops."

Intuitiveness

Your Shiba will quickly learn your moods. When you are tense or stressed, your emotions will travel straight down the leash to your Shiba. She will react to your emotions in ways that are positive and negative. If you are sad or unhappy, your Shiba will approach you with kisses or stay close to your side. The Shiba is not clingy by nature, but when you are upset, she will be there for you. When you are busy or preoccupied, your Shiba will leave you alone. If you approach a Shiba in a fearful or tentative manner, she may adopt the behavior of a bully. The Shiba needs to know her owner is in control. She is like a receiver, with your emotions acting as signals. The signals you send will be received and are often amplified by your Shiba.

Playfulness

The Shiba is playful by nature. She is a willing partner in a game of catch or she will entertain herself with a toy for hours. Many Shibas will give you your exercise with the game "catch me if you can." Remember the strong "play drive" of the Shiba when you are training. If your Shiba is having fun or participating in a game, she is much more involved and receptive to learning. Be creative—almost any training exercise can be turned into a game. Your Shiba enjoys few things more than sharing playtime with her family.

Intelligence

The Shiba is a very intelligent breed. She will quickly adapt to your environment and take over the household immediately. Shibas are observant and receptive. A Shiba owner finds out quickly that he or she needs to be continually one step ahead of his or her Shiba companion. Shibas possess long memories—once a lesson is learned, it seldom needs to be retaught. Conversely, a negative experience is remembered as well. Take care that your Shiba has positive experiences while she is young. It can prove difficult to overcome stimuli that produce a negative or fearful experience with your Shiba.

Size

The size of the Shiba makes her a perfect companion for many households. She is not a large breed and is easy to maintain. Exercise requirements are moderate in smaller dogs, and your Shiba will not need the space or time requirements associated with large breeds. The Shiba is also big enough that it is not a toy breed. She is a hardy dog and can participate with her owners in athletic activities, such as jogging. The Shiba is not a lap dog and is often referred to as a big dog in a small package.

SELECTING YOUR SHIBA INU

The Internet is a valuable source of information. If you don't have a computer, you may wish to take a trip to the local library to assist you in your search. You will find many interesting articles and breeder web sites.

Finding a Breeder

Please keep in mind the famous expression, "caveat emptor"—let the buyer beware. The Internet is a great way to gather information, but it is not advisable to purchase a puppy sight unseen from a web site. Research the breeder's credentials and speak with him or her directly. You are making a long-term commitment to your new family member, not to mention a significant financial investment. Nothing can replace a visit with the breeder and adult Shibas to give you peace of mind that the new addition to your family is a healthy puppy with a sound temperament.

The AKC and the NSCA provide an excellent Breeder Referral Program (see Information). These resources will help to match you with a reputable breeder in your area. Shibas are not a common breed and you may have to drive several hours to meet with a breeder. The trip is generally well worth it. This is an excellent opportunity to meet the adult Shiba. Puppies are very cute, but they grow up quickly. Spending time with the adults is a great way to make sure the Shiba is the right breed for you. It is also an opportunity for you to meet the breeder, to assess the breeder's willingness to work with you on areas of training, to establish rapport with the breeder, and to evaluate the temperament of the pup's parents.

Meeting the Parents

Many times the breeder will not have the sire or father of a litter at his or her home. The breeder may have selected a male belonging to someone else as the ideal partner to complement the female. This is a common practice and if the male is nearby, the breeder may assist you to make an appointment to meet the father of the puppies or may be able to provide or show you photos of the father. Keep in mind that nature is not kind to the

female of any species during the reproductive process. A Shiba dam or mother does not look her best after having puppies. Nature triggers a coat shed during the whelping process, clearing the belly of hair to facilitate nursing puppies. The Shiba mother with a luxuriant coat a few months earlier now looks naked. A well-known AKC judge is fond of saying, "She came to the party, but left her dress at home" to describe Shibas during the shedding process. At no time is this more apparent than when a dam is nursing puppies. Evaluate the dam of the litter for her temperament, not her appearance. If you pay an additional visit to the breeder in a few months, the mother of your puppy will look like a different dog.

Evaluating the Breeder

When you speak with the breeder, don't be surprised if you feel the breeder is interviewing you; he or she probably is. It is important to most breeders that the puppies they place go to good homes. Look for breeders who:

✔ Take time to discuss the breed with you.

✔ Make the commitment to work with you throughout the training process and the entire life of the dog.

✔ Are willing to discuss health problems in the breed (see Keeping Your Shiba Inu Healthy and Well Groomed) and inform you of the level of health screening done on the parents, such as for eye disorders, subluxating patellas, and hip dysplasia.

✔ Find out about you and your needs, instead of focusing on their status or accomplishments.

✔ Respect the breed clubs and are not openly hostile and disparaging of the other breeders in their area.

✔ Enjoy the breed, are passionate about the breed, and speak highly of the breed in general. This is not to say they shouldn't warn you of potential drawbacks.

✔ Focus on whether you and a Shiba puppy are a good fit, instead of centering on asking you to send a check.

A reputable breeder is your strongest support system. His or her role is to help and guide you through the training process. The breeder should discuss potential drawbacks to Shiba ownership, as well as the positive points. The Shiba Inu is a breed in which early socialization is essential. A significant percentage of the Shibas that are turned into shelters or are placed in rescue with temperament problems were not adequately socialized as puppies. New owners must be educated properly on how to train and raise a Shiba. Reputable breeders work diligently to breed healthy puppies of sound temperament.

Breeding dogs is a time consuming and expensive hobby when done correctly. Breeders invest significant time researching bloodlines to match parents that hopefully produce offspring of sound mind and body. A good breeder is active in the sport of purebred dogs, not just to compete and have her offspring evaluated by judges, but to observe the traits of the other dogs in the ring to evaluate the strengths and weakness of other bloodlines. The breeder screens for genetic diseases and inherited conditions that affect the quality of life of parents and potential offspring. The breeder tracks and records traits occurring within his or her lines and the effects produced when combining the lines with other lines and pedigrees.

The reputable breeder stands behind any puppy he or she has brought into this world, and will take back, regardless of the circumstances, at any point in the life of the dog. The reputable breeder is prepared to spend hours training and socializing puppies as well as training and educating Shiba owners to offer a support system for people experiencing difficulties with their Shiba.

What to Consider

Puppy or Adult?

If you have made the decision that the Shiba Inu is the right breed for your family, the next decision is to select an individual companion. Traditional wisdom suggests the adoption of a puppy. A puppy is a relatively clean slate and training begins from scratch. This approach works well and the first experience with a Shiba for most new owners is with a puppy. However, if your experience in training is limited, another option to consider is adopting an adult.

Many breeders are willing to place retired show dogs with new owners. These older dogs have matured through the difficult puppy phase and are often an ideal companion for the inexperienced owner. Additionally, there are many Rescue Organizations (see Information) that have adults available for adoption. Your contact in Rescue will tell you the strengths of the dog, as well as any developmental issues. In either case, you have an experienced contact that will help you and the dog through any transitional issues.

If you are up to the challenge of raising a puppy, the next step is to prepare for the new addition to the family. Begin by discussing the ground rules with each member of the family. Compile a list of ideal traits and basic expectations you have for the puppy both as an adolescent and an adult. Also, create a list of forbidden activities.

Compare the lists of ideal traits and forbidden activities for each member of the family. Are there conflicts between the family member's lists? For example, Mom's list includes keeping the dog off the furniture as a forbidden activity, while one of the children list having the dog sleep with him as a desirable activity. Discuss any conflicting expectations and resolve them before bringing the newest family member home. If you don't want your adult Shiba sleeping in bed with you, make the decision early and train accordingly.

Male or Female?

It is important to meet the adults of the breed to determine if you are interested in selecting a male or female companion. Most of the discussion will focus on intact Shibas, in other words, males that are not neutered and females that are not spayed. Keep in mind that spaying or neutering young will alter these behaviors. The effect of spaying and neutering on gender distinctions is discussed in the chapter "Keeping Your Shiba Inu Healthy and Well Groomed."

The breed displays very different characteristics between the males and the females. Most of the literature available on the breed describes the adult male. Males bond closely with their owners and form deep attachments. They can be protective of their family and are often aloof with strangers. Adult males should not show aggression to strangers. Rather, they are often indifferent. They look at strangers and seem to say, "Hmmm, you have never played with me, and you don't feed me. I don't see any reason to fawn all over you." Most adult males have a strong sense of dignity and can't be bothered with the stranger who wants to pet or hold them, but bring out a tennis ball or squeaky toy and the situation often changes radically. The stranger is now a good friend who is offering to accommodate his interests. Some adult males may not take well to small children. Small children, toddlers in particular, have no respect for the dignity of the male. Toddlers do not hesitate to pull tails or ears, poke eyes, climb on backs, or take away food or toys. Many adult males do not have patience with this behavior. Finally, Shibas are very clean dogs, but some males will begin marking their territory if they are not neutered prior to reaching adult or sexual maturity.

Females tend to display a willingness to greet strangers, and are often the social butterflies. The adult female believes everyone who enters your home has done so to entertain her. She will present visitors with toys and pester them to play with her. If this doesn't work she may jump on their lap and indulge in various antics to assure that she remains the center of attention. Females are more patient with children, with one significant exception. When a female is in estrus or has young puppies, she may lose her patience with strangers and children. She may view children as a potential threat to her puppies and her behavior will change temporarily. In general, Shiba females do not understand the term "stranger." They will happily leave with any person wielding a tennis ball or squeaky toy.

Dog aggression: Shibas in general have a tendency toward dog aggression. The males tend to posture more than the females, and give more warning of a potential problem. Males may "trash talk," barking or growling at another dog, while the female will often jump into a dog fight without advance warning.

Even if your Shiba does not start a confrontation with another dog, she will probably not back down if challenged, regardless of the size of the other dog. The Shiba does not understand she is a small dog. Shibas were bred to hunt the wild boar, which is several times the size of a Shiba. This breed, throughout its history in Japan, did not hesitate to challenge a boar and today will not hesitate to take on a significantly larger dog if challenged. Early correction of aggressive behavior and socialization utilizing programs such as a puppy kindergarten class can make a significant difference in the Shiba's ability to get along with other dogs.

Other dogs: If you already have a dog and the Shiba will become the second dog in the household, seriously consider choosing a Shiba of a different gender than the dog you have at home. Shibas work best in male-female pairs and generally get along best in this combination. Two males or two females in the household may get along, but it generally requires significant work and experienced dog owners to establish a harmonious relationship.

Color

Many people interested in adding a Shiba to their family have never seen a Shiba in person—they found the breed in a book or on a web site. For this reason, many people are not aware that the breed comes in four colors. Three colors are preferred for exhibiting the Shiba at conformation dog shows: red, red sesame, and black and tan. Shibas also come in cream color. While the cream color is a serious fault in the show ring, it is not tied to any known genetic health defects and should not be viewed as a drawback for a companion pet. The web site for the National Shiba Club of America (see Information) illustrates the three preferred colors. While you may have a specific color in mind, remember, color is a cosmetic trait. Temperament is a more important consideration when selecting a companion you will live with for many years to come. The more specific you are about the puppy you want, the more patience you must exercise in waiting for a puppy to arrive that meets your specifications.

Limited Choices

Litter size is relatively small in the Shiba Inu; the average litter contains three puppies. You may not have the option of choosing a puppy from the entire litter. Most reputable breeders actively participate in the

sport of purebred dogs by showing their dogs in the conformation ring. A breeder plans each litter carefully, usually with the plan to keep a puppy from that breeding to provide a stepping-stone to the next generation of his or her breeding program. For this reason, the breeder may have one or more of the puppies in the litter slated for show homes. The breeder may make only a few puppies available to qualified pet homes.

The breeder will work with the puppy during the first eight weeks and observe the traits of the individual puppy's temperament. He or she may determine that a particular puppy requires a home without children or needs a single-dog environment. Most breeders, having met you and your family, will work with you to find the best puppy for your situation. The puppy that provides the best match for your family may not meet your specifications for color or gender. If you are flexible you will find the right puppy sooner. However, if you have your heart set on a specific color and gender, exercise patience. It may take a while for your breeder to find the right puppy for your family. Don't sacrifice temperament or ignore the breeder's advice just to have a puppy immediately. You are making a commitment of 14 to 16 years to your puppy—longer than the average

marriage in the United States today. Make sure the puppy's personality is a good fit for your family. Shiba ownership is a wonderful experience when personalities are matched correctly; however, a personality mismatch provides a trying experience for your family as well as for the puppy.

Breeder Contracts and Guarantees

Most reputable breeders require and provide a contract to adopt a Shiba puppy. If you are not active in the sport of purebred dogs, most breeders will require that you agree to spay or neuter your companion pet. You will most likely find this a contractual condition of adoption. Many breeders will require you to meet other conditions. Typical requirements are

✔ Keep the puppy up-to-date on all vaccinations
✔ Schedule annual veterinary visits
✔ Maintain the Shiba on year-round heartworm preventative
✔ Prevent external parasites, such as fleas or ticks
✔ Prevent internal parasites
✔ Microchip the puppy
✔ Provide adequate food and shelter
✔ Keep the puppy in safe and humane conditions.

Individual contracts vary, but the conditions for adoption are similar.

Most breeders comply with the laws in their area, and will most often extend the legal requirements. You should receive a guarantee that the puppy is healthy. Take your puppy to a veterinarian within a few days of bringing the puppy home. If your veterinarian discovers that the puppy is ill or has a serious defect the breeder did not disclose to you, contact the breeder immediately. You should return the puppy and the breeder should refund your money or replace the puppy. If you wish to keep the puppy, the breeder may return a portion of the purchase price to compensate for the problem.

Most breeders offer extended guarantees. Dogs are generally warranted to be free of serious genetic defects until they reach two years of age. Most developmental defects will occur prior to this time. Perhaps the most important indication of the ethics of your breeder is his or her willingness to stand behind his or her dogs. Most breeders allow you to return the dog to them at any time during the dog's life. If your circumstances change, or if behavioral problems occur, most breeders are willing to have you return the dog to them. They will work to retrain unacceptable behavior or locate a new home for the dog, if required. However, it is not the breeder's fault if you are required to move to a new home that won't allow dogs or if your circumstances change, and generally behavioral problems occur as a result of inadequate or improper training. For these reasons, most breeders do not offer to buy back the dog, but they are willing to have the dog returned to them to assure that it has a qualified new home or to make sure the behavioral problems are corrected.

PREPARING FOR
YOUR SHIBA INU

*Once you have made the commitment
to add a Shiba to your family
and have selected your puppy,
the next important step is to
prepare your home for the
new arrival.*

Getting Ready for Your Puppy

Prepare your home for a puppy before bringing the puppy home. Determine where the puppy will receive her exercise. Do you plan to walk the puppy on leash or do you have a fenced area for the puppy to run and explore? If you plan to walk the Shiba on leash, consider acquiring a harness or a martingale leash. A buckle collar is a great way to provide identification and the Shiba can wear it at all times; however, the shape of the Shiba head allows a standard buckle collar to slip over the head quite easily. While walking, if the Shiba balks and comes to a stop, you may find you are holding onto the leash with the collar attached and the Shiba running free in the opposite direction. Shibas seem to take to the leash-breaking process much easier with a harness; however, some Shibas learn quickly to back

out of the harness. Often a Shiba will fight and struggle with the leash and collar. If you wish to try using the leash and collar approach, a nylon choke collar provides more security while walking your dog. The nylon collar is used in conjunction with the buckle collar. After the walk, remove the nylon collar. This type of collar tightens with pressure. If it is caught on something it may strangle the dog; therefore have the dog wear it only while you are there to supervise.

Fencing

If you have a fenced area, check the fence line for areas that may require repair. A fence provides a good barrier for short periods. A fence is not a good baby-sitter. Shibas are naturally curious and were bred to hunt. A squirrel running on the fence may provide the incentive for a Shiba to jump over the fence, climb the fence like a ladder, or to dig an escape route under the fence. If you need to leave the Shiba outside for extended periods, a covered run on a concrete pad will minimize the opportunity for escape. Keep in mind that extended periods on concrete are hard on the joints, and are not a particularly good environment for developing puppies and older or geriatric dogs with arthritis.

Many people have had positive experiences with invisible fences. If you opt for this approach, consult with the manufacturer to determine the best way to train your dog to the perimeter.

A word of caution: While an invisible fence may keep your dog in your yard, it provides no barrier for other animals entering your yard. If another animal enters your yard and a chase ensues, the Shiba may not consider the jolt she can receive enough incentive to keep her from breaking the barrier when she is caught up in the thrill of the chase.

Sleeping Arrangements

Something else to consider before bringing the puppy home is where she is going to sleep. Many people like to sleep with their dogs. If this is your wish, you may want to consider beginning by setting up a crate in the bedroom. Once the housetraining process is complete, allow the dog free run

of the bedroom and bring her up on the bed at bedtime.

Other people enjoy their dogs, but do not wish to sleep with them. If this is your situation, find a comfortable area in your home that is warm and dry in which to set up a crate for your puppy.

Finding a Veterinarian

A most important step is to locate a veterinarian. Consult with your breeder, friends, family, and neighbors for a recommended veterinarian. Find out if he or she has experience with Shibas or if he or she is comfortable working with the breed. Determine the hours of operation for the practice and if someone is on call for emergencies. If the veterinarian is not on call after hours, find out where the practice refers emergencies. If the emergency facility is a considerable drive, you may want to consider a practice with on call emergency services.

Training Programs

Investigate the local training programs. Again, breeders, friends, family, and neighbors are a great source of information. Find out if the instructor has experience with Shibas and if the class schedule meets your work and family requirements. Training and motivating a Shiba is a unique experience, and different training techniques may become necessary. Ask the instructor about his or her flexibility in training.

Puppy-proofing Your Home

Puppy-proofing your home is an essential element in preparing for your puppy. Compare the checklist provided here to items in your household. Remove any items on the list from the house or place them out of reach of the puppy.

Electrical cords and telephone cables are favorite toys and are particularly dangerous for a teething puppy. Puppies are also fond of items that carry their owner's scent. Socks and underwear become prized possessions. These items are a hazard to the puppy if ingested, not to mention a social embarrassment when the puppy

═CHECKLIST═

Hazards to Your Pet
✔ Chocolate
✔ Cleaning products and antifreeze
✔ Poisonous plants
✔ Electrical cords
✔ Small or easily ingested objects

trots them out to present to guests. Breakables, valuables, and sentimental possessions should be moved beyond the puppy's reach.

Shopping List

If you have time, visit a local pet store to determine what items are available. Compare the prices at the local pet store with mail order options. Each of the shopping list items is discussed in detail in subsequent chapters.

Food and Nutritional Supplies
✔ Food bowl and water bucket
✔ Puppy food
✔ Vitamins and supplements
✔ Treats

Housing Requirements
✔ Crate
✔ Bedding

Exercise Tools
✔ Harness
✔ Buckle collar
✔ Nylon leashes
✔ Nylon choke collar

Grooming Supplies
✔ Pin brush
✔ Slicker brush
✔ Rubber curry
✔ Metal comb
✔ Shampoo
✔ Nail clippers or grinder

Toys
✔ Tennis ball
✔ Squeaky toys
✔ Dental bones and rawhide chews

AT HOME WITH YOUR SHIBA INU

You've found a breeder, selected your puppy, and prepared your home; now it's time to bring your new puppy home.

Bringing Your Puppy Home

When you make the trip to your breeder to pick up your puppy, be sure to bring a crate. Many crates are designed with your Shiba's safety in mind during car and airplane travel. Traveling in the car with a puppy running loose is dangerous to you and your puppy. If you are involved in an automobile accident, not only does the crate offer your puppy protection from injury, the crate prevents your puppy from escaping and running loose on the highway, at a time when you may have injuries and other serious matters requiring your attention.

The New Environment

Your puppy is about to experience her new home. Sights and scents are different and nothing will seem familiar to her. While many Shibas waltz into a new home and claim it immediately, some experience anxiety and stress. Your puppy may seem fearful, hiding under a couch, trembling, or she may even try to avoid contact with her new family members by running away from them. Provide comfort and take heart; this behavior should pass within a few days. If it continues beyond a few days contact your breeder. He or she may have some suggestions to ease the transition.

If your puppy appears afraid of you or other household members beyond four weeks, the puppy is having a difficult time adjusting to her new home and the stress of changing environments may not ease. Contact your breeder; for some reason the puppy is not adjusting to her new home and you may wish to discuss other options, such as trying a different puppy.

For many families there is great excitement in bringing home the new puppy and the desire to share your excitement with friends and family is strong. Resist the temptation to have a

TIP

Car Sickness

Ask your breeder not to feed your puppy prior to you bringing your Shiba home. A heavy stomach may cause your puppy to experience car sickness. Waiting until you get home to feed your puppy reduces the likelihood of car sickness and gives you a good opportunity to provide comfort when you feed your hungry Shiba.

full house waiting for your new arrival. Make the transition a calm and tranquil experience. Loud noises and high levels of activity can add more stress to an already stressful experience. You will have plenty of time after your Shiba has adjusted to her new home to introduce her to family and friends. The typical curious Shiba is more than ready to explore her new home, but keep in mind that she has just left her family and may experience some anxiety.

Housetraining

The Crate

There are a variety of methods for you to consider when housetraining your Shiba puppy. Shibas are very clean dogs and perhaps the easiest method for housetraining your Shiba is to begin the process with crate training. Crate training works by using your Shiba's instinctive cleanliness coupled with the early training your puppy received from her mother and breeder. A wild dog will find a den for herself. Providing your

Shiba with a crate for her home is like providing her with a den. The typical clean Shiba, even as a puppy, will try to avoid soiling her home.

1. Before you begin your morning routine, pick your Shiba up from her crate and carry her outside to the area you have designated for her to relieve herself.

2. Place your puppy on the ground and allow her to move around and explore. More than likely, she will take advantage of the opportunity quite quickly. Allow plenty of time for her to both urinate and defecate.

3. Bring your puppy indoors and allow her a few minutes to explore her home. Afterward, return her to the crate and provide the morning meal.

4. Give your puppy about ten minutes to eat and then pick her up and carry her outside again.

A young puppy does not have the control she will have as an adult and frequent visits outside will reduce accidents in the crate. Always allow your puppy an opportunity to go outside shortly after eating and before you settle her in for the night. In a very short time, your Shiba puppy will understand where her area is and she will extend the respect she has for her crate to the rest of your home.

Note: Your puppy may have been making a valiant effort to not spoil her crate. As soon as her feet touch the ground outside of the crate, she will search for an area to "take care of business." Carrying your puppy outdoors reduces indoor accidents and reinforces to your puppy where she is allowed to relieve herself. Additionally, using the same door each time you take your puppy outside reinforces the housetraining process. Before long your puppy will be telling you when she needs to go outside by approaching or watching the door.

Paper training: Many training techniques use paper training as an interim step in the housetraining process. This step is not only unnecessary with the Shiba, it is not desired. It is much better to teach your Shiba to go outside immediately. Breaking the Shiba of eliminating indoors, once taught, may prove difficult or impossible.

Socialization and Training

Socializing your Shiba puppy begins with introducing your puppy to the other members of your household. Introducing your Shiba to the adults of the household is easy and usually involves toys and treats, but introducing the Shiba to children and other pets requires more planning and effort.

Children

Explain the needs of a young puppy to children who are old enough to understand and manage introductions carefully. Any inappropriate or aggressive behavior requires immediate correction. Introducing a new puppy to infants or toddlers is an important introduction that requires advance planning. Explain to your toddler that he or she must be gentle with the puppy. If you are introducing an infant, note that there will not be significant interaction between infant and puppy at this stage in the life of your infant. The main purpose of the introduction is to make the puppy aware that the infant is also a part of her new family. This type of introduction is brief and controlled. The puppy may think you are offering her a toy or playmate and the experience may prove frightening to the infant. Your Shiba will discover your infant in the course of day-to-day activities and will observe your behavior with your young family members to gauge her behavior accordingly.

Other Pets

Introducing your Shiba puppy to existing household pets needs to be done with common sense and forethought. Remove items such as food or toys that are likely to promote conflict. Shibas generally react well with other dogs and cats if introduced as a puppy. These animals will often sort out their hierarchy all by themselves without your intervention. However, aggressive or inappropriate behavior needs immediate correction. Your Shiba must understand that she is not allowed to bully the other animals and vice versa. After the introductions are complete, you will still need to monitor interaction for quite some time. Even though they may play nicely when introduced, conflict can develop quickly and you need to be prepared to intervene for the protection of your pets. For this reason, until you are comfortable that the relationship between your pets is a stable one, it is a good idea to separate the pets when they are unattended.

Shibas may not interact with pets that could be construed as prey, such as birds, hamsters, ferrets, or other small animals. Introducing your Shiba to these types of pets requires common sense and should be avoided. Your Shiba will understand in time that there are members of the household she is not allowed to play with or bother. Many Shibas live peacefully with a variety of small animals, but each has his or her own space and rarely are they companions.

Training Programs

You have many options available for socializing your Shiba puppy with other animals. Many communities offer puppy kindergarten programs, obedience programs, or dog parks. Other community activities where dogs are allowed, such as soccer games, provide a great opportunity to interact with different people as well as other animals.

Patience and Consistency

Training a Shiba can prove to be a challenging experience. The innate intelligence of the Shiba when coupled with a strong and independent nature creates a situation where the Shiba needs incentive to follow your commands, instead of following her own inclinations. Patience and consistency are the most important components of any training program with the ultimate goal of raising a well-behaved Shiba. Shibas don't respond well to loud voices or to harsh jerks on the leash; however, it is important not to go too far in the other direction. A Shiba will take advantage of every opportunity. Firmness tempered with gentleness is an absolute must. Resist the temptation to beg your dog to perform by constantly repeating commands, the whole

TIP

Comfort Blanket or Towel

Send a blanket or towel to your breeder a few weeks before you bring your puppy home. Ask the breeder to rub the puppy's dam and littermates with the towel. Bring the blanket home with the puppy and place it in her crate when you arrive at home. Don't use this blanket for the car ride home as, if your Shiba experiences an upset stomach and the blanket needs cleaning, you will have defeated the purpose for bringing it home. Scents that are familiar can provide comfort the first few nights your puppy is in her new home.

while feeding her treats. Try a middle-of-the-road approach. Your goal is to earn your Shiba's respect while training her to obey your commands in a manner that is successful without instilling behaviors that may be difficult to repair.

Learning Her Name

Start the segment of the training process in your home where there are fewer distractions than outdoors. Use your puppy's name frequently during feeding and play. Frequent repetition of her name will begin to produce recognition and a positive response.

Play: Your first goal should be to get your puppy's attention for an extended period of time. Shibas love to play and using this drive to facilitate training speeds up the process. Get a ball or toy and call your puppy's name. At this stage it doesn't matter what her body is doing as long as she's looking directly at you or the toy, with her ears up and without shifting interest. When your Shiba responds, give her the toy and praise her, using her name.

Food: Another technique to assist with name recognition uses food. Prior to giving your puppy her meals, call her name. When you have her attention and she approaches you give her the food. Between meals, call her name and offer her a treat or biscuit. When you have her attention and she has responded to her name, give her the treat. Perform this exercise several times a day. If you call her name frequently and offer her food, a treat, or toy, she will begin responding to you when you call her name.

The Come Command

1. Begin by using easy-to-break dog cookies or a similar type of treat. Give the puppy a tiny bit of the cookie to gain her attention.

2. Once she has finished it, put the cookie in front of her nose to let her know you have more.

3. When you have your Shiba's attention, raise the cookie out of her reach (bending forward far enough so that she can't jump onto your legs) for about three seconds.

4. Step back and use your puppy's name with the *come* command; call her to you and give her the treat and plenty of praise.

Keep treats and toys nearby and practice the *come* command any time you aren't busy. Once your Shiba is coming to you and responding to her name indoors, you're ready to work with her outdoors where there are more distractions.

Outdoors: Have your toys and treats handy and begin the next step by training in an enclosed area outdoors. Repeat the same exer-

TIP

Collars

A buckle collar made of rolled leather works well as it won't damage the coat, and is very gentle on the neck. A flat nylon collar may wear away the soft puppy coat underneath, and a choke collar should never be left on any dog, especially a puppy.

cises as above until your Shiba reliably comes to you when she is called. Next try the exercises without food or toys, but continue praising her when she obeys a command.

If your Shiba takes the opportunity to explore the outdoor environment and doesn't come when called or tries to initiate a game of "catch me, if you can," try the exercises with a leash. Some Shibas may be willing to *come* to get a treat or toy, but when you want to pick her up or bring her inside, she may dart out of the way. When your Shiba plays this game with you, she is showing you that she is willing to *come* to you when she wants to and that she understands your command, but she is resisting your commands in an effort to impose her will. Gently but firmly enforce your command using the leash to bring the Shiba to you.

Leash Training

Several tools and techniques are available for leash training your puppy. Gather your tools: identification collar (rolled leather or flat nylon), retractable leash (16 foot [4.9 m]), short leash (4–6 foot [1.4–1.8 m]), toys, treats, and either a harness or nylon choke collar. You will be introduced to the training process using the leash and collar approach; however, if you are using a harness, follow the process by substituting the harness for the training collar.

1. Begin by allowing your puppy to become accustomed to the restraint of her identification collar. You'll notice when you first put a collar on the Shiba baby (unless the breeder has already trained her to wear a collar) that she will toss her head, stop every few steps to shake and scratch, etc. Shibas do not appreciate this sort of restriction and she may even begin to scream as though she is hurt or injured. Pay no attention to her antics and attempts to remove the collar. Put the collar on, being certain that it fits snugly, but not too tight. A good fit is when you can easily insert two fingers between the puppy's neck and the collar. Remember that a Shiba's neck is usually as big as or bigger than her head, so it must be snug enough not to slip off over her head, but not so tight as to choke her. Once the collar is properly fitted and in place, let the puppy wear it until she no longer resents it. This may take a few days.

2. The next step is to attach the leash. In the early stages of the leash-breaking process a lightweight, 16-foot (4.9-m) retractable leash works well. Work with the leash in your left hand, to train your Shiba to walk on your left. Allow your Shiba puppy to use as much of the leash as she wants to use. Some puppies will flail around like a fish out of water—just stand quietly by and let her flail. Resist the temptation to sympathize with her or speak to her harshly; it is best not to say anything until she's over her tantrum. Make sure the leash never gets tight. Some puppies will try

to outrun the leash; in this case, just run along behind her, keeping up with her so the leash doesn't get tight. Other puppies will refuse to move at all; get comfortable and wait her out. It's very important that the puppy feels no tension on the leash. Once she does start moving, tell her how wonderful she is and keep up with her. Training sessions should last no more than 10 to 15 minutes, but can be repeated several times in a day.

3. After a couple of days of following her around, you're ready to start teaching the puppy to go with you, rather than following her. Use one of your Shiba's favorite toys or food to coax her. Show her the toy or food and walk away about 5 or 6 feet (1.5–1.8 m)—no tension on the leash—without looking at her, but encouraging her constantly with your voice. If she comes with you, reward her by giving her the toy for a few seconds to play with or give her the food to eat. If she doesn't come with you, bend down, showing her the

she keeps pace at your side. Speak to your Shiba while you are walking, frequently praising her efforts. Use this process to reinforce your Shiba's response to her name: "*Good girl,*" only substitute your Shiba's name for girl. Stop frequently and encourage your Shiba to rest at your side. Offer a small treat or toy as a reward to reinforce the lesson. Repeat the *heel* command and begin walking forward. Short and frequent sessions work best when training a Shiba. Four 15-minute sessions per day will have your Shiba walking on the leash and *heeling* at your side within a few weeks.

Hint: Slice a hot dog into several round slices. Quarter the hot dog rounds into small pieces. Place the hot dog pieces in a plastic bag (to protect your clothing) and then put the plastic bag in your left pocket. As you are walking with your puppy, give her a piece of the hot dog frequently to reinforce her good behavior. The hot dog pieces are small and consumed quickly and your Shiba puppy will not be distracted by taking the time to consume a larger biscuit. You will notice that your Shiba puppy is walking at your side, watching your left pocket for her reward—voilà, *heeling* at your left side, attentively watching you. No one needs to know your well-behaved Shiba is really watching your pocket for a treat.

toy or food and encourage her to come to you. When she gets there, give her the reward and praise her lavishly. Repeat this process three or four times and then stop. Give your Shiba at least an hour before repeating the training session, but this also can be practiced several times a day.

4. On the seventh or eighth day (if you've been practicing every day) you're ready to go to a short leash (4 to 6 feet [1.2–1.8 m]). Repeat the session above, being careful to keep the leash loose. Talk to your puppy encouragingly the entire time so she will keep her head up. Remember to reward her often.

Heeling

Once your Shiba will walk along with you without protest it's time to introduce the process of *heeling*. You want to teach her to respond to the traditional *heel* command. Begin by saying *"Heel"* and then start walking forward briskly, keeping the leash loose, while

The Sit, Stand, Down, and Stay Commands

After your puppy is *heeling* at your side, you are ready to begin adding a few more commands to her repertoire.

1. Using what your puppy has already learned, attach the leash and begin walking forward several steps after giving your puppy the *heel* command.

2. Come to a stop and say *"Stand."* Offer her a treat, giving it to her only after she is standing on all four feet and paying attention to you. Praise lavishly when your puppy follows your commands.

3. Next, say *"Heel"* and take several steps forward. Come to a stop and tuck her into a *sit,* as you use the command *"Sit."* Give her a treat and praise her.

4. Repeat the process: Begin walking forward giving the *heel* command, come to a stop, and alternate between the *stand* and *sit* command. Your puppy is learning all three of the fundamental obedience commands (*heel, sit,* and *stand*) at once. Whether she does it or not, she is quite well aware of what is expected. Remember, Shibas can be quite stubborn when they've had enough. Short, frequent sessions are more successful than long extended training sessions.

Once your puppy has mastered the three basic commands, it is time for her to learn the *down* command.

1. Bring your puppy into a sitting position. Have a treat in your right hand and show it to her.

2. Place your left hand on your puppy's shoulder and firmly but gently press down while saying *"Down."*

3. Once your puppy is in the *down* position, reward her with the treat and praise her success. Repeat this exercise for several days, and then begin giving the *down* command from a *stand* as well as from *sit.*

Another successful technique for teaching the *down* command is to coax her down with food.

1. Begin with your puppy in the *sit* position. Move to the front of the dog and show her a treat.

2. Bend down bringing the treat to the floor. Issue the *down* command. Once your puppy is in the *down* position, give her the treat and praise her achievement. If your puppy can't be coaxed into the *down* position, place your hand on her shoulder and press down gently while giving the *down* command. Again, once she is in the *down* position, give her a reward and praise her.

3. Occasionally when using this technique your puppy will lunge forward to get the treat. If she is doing this, spend a little more time on the *sit* command before moving on to the *down* command. If she is holding the *sit* command without breaking for food, she is ready to use this technique for the *down* command.

Stay is often the most difficult command to teach a Shiba. Your Shiba may begin the process successfully; however, at some point she will realize she has a choice: to obey your command or to take the opportunity to escape to do something she wants to do. For the safety of your Shiba, use a long retractable or training leash for this exercise. If your Shiba breaks the command, you will still have control of your puppy.

1. Begin by placing your Shiba in a sitting position. Firmly say *"Stay"* and walk about 10 feet (3 m) away. If your Shiba gets up to leave,

give the *sit* command followed immediately by the *stay* command.

2. Begin by leaving her in the *stay* position for between 5 and 10 seconds.

3. After your puppy has *stayed* for the desired length of time, issue the *come* command, recalling your Shiba to your side.

4. Repeat frequently, alternating between the *sit* and the *down* command to begin the exercise. Extend the time length for your *stay* command gradually.

Mouthing or Biting

Puppies learn to communicate with their littermates by mouthing. If you observe a litter of puppies you will quickly notice they have their mouths all over each other. This behavior is thought to be a method of communicating as well as establishing the hierarchy or pecking order. If you observe the litter long enough, you will notice a puppy extending this behavior to her mother. Shiba mothers respond quickly and firmly. A bark and a nip put the puppy firmly in her place in the litter hierarchy.

Your Shiba puppy will probably attempt to extend this behavior into her new home. While some think this behavior is cute in a puppy, there is nothing cute about an adult Shiba biting a person. Your Shiba puppy needs to learn immediately that putting her mouth on a human is not acceptable. A firm *"NO!"* accompanied by a squeeze to the muzzle, repeated every time she puts her mouth on a person, will usually eliminate the behavior. A more dominant puppy may require a firmer response. Check early with your veterinarian, breeder, or trainer for suggestions, if you feel your puppy is not responding. If left unchecked, this bid for dominance will escalate into growling or

biting, signs of overt aggression. A common mistake in training a biting or mouthy puppy is to attempt to distract the behavior by giving the puppy a toy or treat. The puppy does not see this as a distraction, but a reward. You will send the message that she will receive a toy or treat when exhibiting dominant behavior; instead of stopping the behavior it will most likely escalate.

The Shiba Scream

Remember that the Shiba is frequently a drama queen. When your Shiba invokes the "Shiba Scream" she is most likely afraid. This blood curdling shriek is one of the hallmarks of the breed. Any Shiba breeder or owner will chuckle when you inquire about this occurrence. When your Shiba emits this high pitched scream, she is providing you with high drama or theater—the response almost always exceeds the stimulus by several orders of magnitude.

Fear

The Shiba will frequently display aggressive behavior when she is afraid. Remember that your Shiba has significant commonality with her ancestor the wolf. A wild animal will react with aggression when cornered. This is a response to a perceived threat or a fear response. It is important to understand the difference between dominance aggression and fear aggression when raising a Shiba puppy. When your Shiba is afraid she will need your reassurance that the fear inducing situation is not a significant threat. Fear aggression, when dealt with using dominance aggression techniques, reinforces the puppy's fear and frequently results in an escalation of the aggressive behavior.

Identification

Shibas are well known for their talent for escaping. If your Shiba gets loose, your chances of having your pet returned to you improve greatly if she has been permanently identified. The two most common methods for permanently identifying dogs are tattoos or microchips.

A tattoo provides permanent identification, but it may not be practical for a Shiba. The Shiba's skin is tough and resistant. Couple this with your Shiba's flair for drama and it may be necessary to anesthetize your Shiba to apply the tattoo. Additionally, as your Shiba's fur grows, a tattoo is often difficult to see. For these reasons, a microchip is often the practical solution to permanently identify your Shiba.

Ask your veterinarian about a microchip. The microchip is about the size of a grain of rice and is generally placed under the loose skin between your Shiba's shoulder blades. This is a simple procedure that does not require anesthesia; however, many veterinarians suggest the procedure accompany spaying or neutering at a time when your puppy is already anesthetized.

Exercise

Your Shiba will gladly accompany you on a long walk or run; however, her exercise needs are moderate. A typical Shiba will meet her daily exercise requirements playing in the house or yard. Shibas are often active, but are rarely hyperactive. They are seldom mindlessly active and are not usually pacers. Your Shiba will engage in activity with a purpose; often related to play or companionship. While some Shibas are couch potatoes, requiring you to provide more frequent walks, this is not typical Shiba behavior.

Children and the Shiba Inu

Most Shibas love children and are excellent companions; however, there is a caveat with this statement. The type of companion your Shiba will be with children is often a direct result of her early training. Shibas must be taught that their place in the family hierarchy is below all humans. If untrained, Shibas frequently view children as equals or subordinates. If managed and trained correctly while she is young, your Shiba will prove to be a dedicated, loving, and loyal companion to your children.

Young children are often rough or fearful with a new puppy. Either situation needs to be managed carefully. Children need to understand that they must take care not to hurt or tease the new puppy. Shibas have long memories. If a puppy is teased, she may not take action while she is young, but at some time when she is feeling more confident, she will assert herself, usually with a behavior that is exaggerated or inappropriate.

Children need to be taught to be comfortable with a new puppy. Children who are afraid of dogs send a signal to the dog that something is not right. A Shiba will sense fear and may attempt to bully or dominate the child. Creating a good relationship between your Shiba puppy and your fearful child requires patience and work. One approach that works well is to allow the child and the puppy to complete an obedience course together. This provides an opportunity for the child and Shiba to bond under the supervision of an individual trained to work with dogs, who will recognize the dog's body language to train out problems as they occur.

Regardless of any special needs of either the Shiba or the child, consistent parental management and training is the key ingredient to forming a loving friendship between children and Shibas.

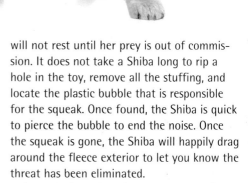

Toys

Shibas love their toys and many unlikely items become prized possessions. Toys play an important role in your Shiba's training and socialization. Providing your Shiba with a variety of toys of differing textures will help to safeguard your possessions. While your Shiba is teething, she will chew on various items to remove baby teeth and to help adult teeth break through the surface of the gums. If your Shiba has toys with a stiff or hard texture, you may save wear and tear on table legs and furniture during this process. Shibas are curious and having their own toys to occupy their attention will assist in keeping them from exploring the house and claiming inappropriate items or destroying household items.

Remember, the Shiba has a very strong prey drive. Stuffed squeaky toys may not last very long with the typical Shiba. The curious Shiba will not rest until her prey is out of commission. It does not take a Shiba long to rip a hole in the toy, remove all the stuffing, and locate the plastic bubble that is responsible for the squeak. Once found, the Shiba is quick to pierce the bubble to end the noise. Once the squeak is gone, the Shiba will happily drag around the fleece exterior to let you know the threat has been eliminated.

A word of caution: Shibas can be possessive with toys. If another animal takes a prized possession, an altercation may occur. You may find it necessary to remove certain toys to avoid conflict if your animals are unattended. Also, it is a good idea to start training your Shiba when she is young to relinquish toys upon command. Work with your Shiba by saying *"Drop"* and making her give up toys on demand at a young age. Continue giving the command frequently throughout her life to reinforce her understanding that she must respond to her human family, even if it requires doing something she doesn't like to do.

Shibas make excellent traveling companions. All that is required is generally a travel crate, food, and plenty of water.

Plane

When planning a trip by airplane, make sure to make reservations for your Shiba.

Some adult Shibas will be small enough to travel in the cabin of the plane in a ventilated travel bag, designed for pet travel, that will fit under the seat in front of you. However, some Shibas will be too large to fit under the seat, and you will have to check them with your luggage.

Hints for Travel

If you are planning to travel with your Shiba consider the following:

✔ Plan your trip to take advantage of nonstop or direct flights wherever possible.

✔ If you are planning to travel outside of your country, make sure of the paperwork and immunizations required for your dog to be admitted into your destination country. Pay attention to quarantine laws and other restrictions.

✔ Speak with your veterinarian and make sure you have sufficient quantities of any medications your pet may need. You may want to inquire about a tranquilizer, if you are concerned your Shiba may be anxious. Ask your veterinarian for a health certificate. Many airlines require a certificate stating the acceptable temperature range for your dog and that your dog is healthy.

✔ Make sure your travel crate is airline-approved and the appropriate size. Your Shiba should be able to stand up and turn around. If the crate is too small, your Shiba will have an uncomfortable trip, and if the crate is too big, your Shiba may be tossed

around inside the crate and become injured if you encounter turbulence during your flight.

✔ Include a leash in your carry-on luggage. You may have an opportunity to walk your dog during layovers when you will not be able to get your luggage. This also allows you to walk your dog safely if your luggage is delayed or lost.

✔ Attach a water container to the inside of the crate, with clean fresh water. You may wish to bring bottled water along, to avoid diarrhea from a change in water at your destination.

✔ Don't feed your Shiba before the flight and don't leave food in the crate. Your Shiba will be more comfortable, even if she is a little hungry, than if she has an upset stomach or needs to relieve herself and can't get anyone's attention.

✔ Place a clean blanket or towel in the crate with your Shiba.

✔ Pack a separate bag with food, water, grooming supplies, and toys for your dog. Be sure to include a box of plastic bags so that you can dispose of your Shiba's stools. Also include an extra towel or sheet of plastic to place under the crate when you arrive at your destination.

✔ Tell the flight attendant on each leg of your flight that you are traveling with your dog and ask to be informed when your dog is on the plane.

✔ Pay attention during stops to the outside temperature. A dog sitting on the tarmac for an extended period will dehydrate quickly, especially in warm weather. Extremely cold weather can be a problem as well; however, Shibas are more susceptible to the heat and dehydration than to cold temperatures.

✔ Make reservations for your dog at the time you purchase your tickets. Some connecting flights may not allow space for pets. It is important to know this before you purchase your ticket.

✔ Make sure the hotels you make your reservations with will accept dogs. Find out if they have an area where you can walk your dog or if there is a dog park nearby.

Automobile

Traveling by automobile with your Shiba is less stressful than traveling by airplane, but requires planning just the same. Many of the same suggestions for traveling by airplane apply to traveling by car; however here are a few additional factors to consider:

✔ Plan rest stops carefully. Do not leave your dog locked in a car with the windows rolled up when you stop for meals. You may leave your dog in her crate with the windows down to provide ventilation for short stops. Make sure your dog has water and try to select parking spots for the shade they provide.

✔ Make sure your overnight accommodations are aware you are traveling with a dog. Surprising friends and family who may have allergies or other issues is never a good idea.

✔ Select areas to walk your dog away from major traffic areas, whenever possible. Your dog is in an unfamiliar area and if you drop the leash or your dog gets loose, remember—a rest stop on a major highway can be a difficult place to recover a lost pet.

FEEDING YOUR SHIBA INU

Many good brands of dog food are commercially available. There are also many specialized canine diets, such as raw food diets. Before you invest a lot of time and money in a specialized diet, consult with your veterinarian and breeder to make sure the proposed diet is safe, healthy, and balanced for your Shiba's age and activity level.

Starting Off Right

Bringing a puppy into a new environment is a stressful time. Young puppies are experiencing vaccinations, deworming treatments, rapid growth, as well as a change in the environment. Several of these events can produce diarrhea in a young puppy. A change of food and water at this time may also trigger a bout of diarrhea in the puppy. While you can't do anything about changing water, you can introduce a new food gradually. Obtain a sample of the puppy's current food from your breeder. Begin by feeding a mixture of three parts of the breeder's food and one part of the new food. Next, feed equal parts of the two foods. Finally, mix one part of the breeder's food with three parts of the new food. Each of these steps should be repeated for two days. The transition between foods will take a week, but will minimize the stress on your puppy from the transition.

Puppies should be offered small portions, frequently. You may choose to feed three or four times per day, while your puppy is very young. Portions increase and frequency decreases as your puppy ages. However, in general, give your Shiba puppy as much as she will eat. Shibas are not usually overeaters, and unless your puppy becomes overweight, you may safely continue this practice throughout the life of your Shiba.

Changing Needs

The typical Shiba grows rapidly during the first six months. At birth, the average puppy weighs 8 ounces. By six months of age many Shibas are very close to their adult height.

They will continue to grow, adding weight and some height throughout the next 18 months, but at no other time are they experiencing so many changes in such a short time. Your Shiba's food intake will increase significantly during this period.

During this growth period your puppy needs a well-balanced diet. Her entire system is developing and she needs your help to grow into a healthy mature adult. Vitamins used as a dietary supplement can provide extra nutrients, needed for growth at this time in your puppy's life. Ask your veterinarian or breeder for a recommendation. Watch your puppy for signs, such as ears folding or drooping, dropping in the pastern (foot), or bowing of the bones in her legs, that she may need more from her diet.

Your puppy is still maturing until about two years of age. While her food intake will stabilize as she grows, she will still need a balanced diet to assist with her overall health throughout her lifetime. Once your Shiba is two years old, she will probably benefit from a maintenance diet until she becomes a senior dog, when she will benefit from a senior diet.

Other Factors Affecting Diet

In addition to rapid growth, many factors influence your Shiba's diet. Activity levels vary between dogs and the amount of exercise your Shiba receives will increase or decrease her food requirements. Climate and weather conditions influence her diet. Dogs generally require an increase in food intake during cold winter months. Of course, if your Shiba is a couch potato and spends most of her winter indoors, you may not need to adjust food levels.

TIP

What to Do When Your Shiba Has Diarrhea

Diarrhea is a condition that occurs when your Shiba has loose, frequent, runny, or watery stools. Many factors can cause a Shiba to have diarrhea, and if diarrhea persists you should contact your veterinarian immediately, as one of the more serious side effects from diarrhea is dehydration.

Feeding your Shiba her normal diet when she has diarrhea may irritate her digestive system and prolong a bout of diarrhea. It is important to break this cycle quickly so your dog does not suffer from dehydration.

At the first sign of diarrhea, remove all food and water for 12 hours. After 12 hours, give her several ounces of an oral electrolyte maintenance solution, such as Pedialyte. This will help to hydrate your Shiba, and unlike tap water it will help to restore an electrolyte imbalance that can occur from the diarrhea. Twelve hours later, if the diarrhea has begun to ease, you may begin to introduce her back to food, but in any case continue with the electrolyte solution. Begin with foods that are easy to digest in small quantities. Boiled white rice combined with a bottle of lamb baby food is a good mixture that provides nutrition and is easy for your dog to digest. Another alternative is browned ground beef, drained of all excess fat. Introduce these easy-to-digest solid foods slowly. Your Shiba's stools should begin to become firmer, and after this point you may resume feeding her normal diet.

How Much to Feed

There is no standard rule of thumb on how much to feed your Shiba. The quantity of food is influenced by content (ingredient list) of the food you have selected. A large male, at the top of the height range, will require more food than a smaller female, at the lower end of the height range. Your Shiba's activity level will influence her dietary needs as well. Experiment with the quantity of food you provide. Begin by following the instructions for your Shiba's weight provided on your dog food bag. If your Shiba finishes her food quickly and still appears hungry, increase the amount of food. If she leaves food and doesn't finish her meal, reduce the amount for her next feeding. Using this technique, you will find the right feeding level for the time of year and growth period for your Shiba. Above all, use common sense, and contact your veterinarian with any concerns.

Water

Water is an important ingredient in the diet of a healthy dog. Your Shiba will need fresh water at all times. A large percentage of the content of your Shiba's body is water and is necessary for your pet's health and survival. Water facilitates many of the functions in your Shiba's body, such as the digestive process. Your Shiba is continuously utilizing the water in her system and needs to continually replace these fluids. Loss of fluids can cause illness and result in the death of your Shiba. Pay close attention to the level of her water bowl during hot summer months. During a period of excessive heat, your Shiba can rapidly become dehydrated.

Supply your Shiba with water at all times by keeping a bowl of fresh water where she can get to it easily. Hang a water bucket in her crate or attach a bowl to the crate door when she is in her crate. Pay attention to your Shiba's fluid consumption. Excessive water consumption or drinking too little water can be indicators of certain health problems. If you are concerned with the amount of water your Shiba is drinking, consult your veterinarian.

Picky Eaters

Many Shibas are classified as picky eaters when they are not being picky; they just aren't hungry. The typical Shiba is not an overeater, and will consume only what she needs; however, if your Shiba is losing weight, you may want to have a veterinary examination to make sure other factors are not involved. Remember, losing coat is not losing weight. Your Shiba will look heavier when she has a full coat and slimmer when she is shedding or has shed out her coat.

Adolescent Shibas often go through a gangly period, where they look thin and in fact, lose weight. Some males go off their food for an extended period during adolescence. These adolescents may eat well for a day or two, then fast for a few days, repeating this cycle for a few months. They grow out of this stage, but it is frustrating while it is happening. Often it is necessary to dress up the food. One trick is to add a few tablespoons of rice on top of the food, but if this doesn't work you may find yourself resorting to the "begging and groveling" feeding technique. Take a handful of kibble and present it to your Shiba or feed her from your hand, a few pieces of kibble at a time. Hand-feeding your Shiba may be the only thing that works. Generally, it is not necessary to go to these lengths; your Shiba will eat when she is hungry and ignore food when she isn't.

Many Shiba owners change feeding patterns or try another food when a Shiba continually refuses to eat. Try changing feeding times, or leaving a bowl of food where your Shiba can get to it at night. Sometimes, allowing the Shiba to feed nocturnally will reverse the pattern. You may also try a different brand of dog food, but more than likely you will end up with a cupboard full of partially consumed bags of food. Resist the temptation to change your Shiba's diet to a human diet. This will set a pattern you may have a very hard time reversing. Your Shiba may happily consume cheeseburgers and French fries, but her dietary needs will suffer.

Obesity

If your Shiba becomes overweight, try a reduced-calorie dog food. Reducing the amount of the existing food may work, but is more often not effective. A reduced-calorie food will provide close to the same quantities of food, but the calorie and fat content is lower. Vigilance is required to help a Shiba lose weight. Your hungry Shiba will look to many sources to find food—she will sort through the garbage, climb on counters, and beg for food when she is hungry. You need to be more creative than your Shiba, to look out for her best interests.

Obesity is not as common as Shibas that are underweight, but it does occur with some frequency in the breed. Obesity is almost always the fault of the owner, not the dog. Excessive weight gain is unhealthy and can create structural and internal problems.

Food Allergies

Shibas may experience allergies to some contents of commercial dog foods in the same way that people have allergies to certain foods. Some of the common culprits are corn, soy, and wheat, but just as with people, Shibas can have allergic reactions from multiple sources. Food allergies are often discovered when your Shiba displays a reaction on her skin. Scratching and itching without another obvious source may indicate that your Shiba is reacting to her food. Runny stools or ongoing bouts of diarrhea may be another indicator that your Shiba is experiencing food allergies. If you suspect that your Shiba is experiencing a food allergy, discuss it with your veterinarian and breeder.

Take the ingredient list from your current food to your veterinary appointment. Your veterinarian may suggest one of the brands of dog food that are formulated specifically for dogs with food allergies or after examining the ingredient list, suggest you search for a commercially available food, without specific suspect ingredients. Treating a Shiba with food allergies may involve a process of elimination, trying to locate the source of the allergic reaction through trial and error, or your veterinarian may suggest testing to identify ingredients that are at the root of the problem.

If an alternative diet does not solve the problem, your veterinarian may also suggest medication to suppress or eliminate the allergic response. In extreme cases, or if the dog is older, these medications may be administered throughout the rest of the dog's life to eliminate the discomfort.

Also, a Shiba may have or may develop allergies due to hereditary or environmental factors. For this reason, notify your breeder if your Shiba is experiencing food allergies. Your breeder will find this information valuable for his or her breeding program and may be able to offer helpful suggestions.

Food Aggression

Food is one of the triggers that may invoke aggressive behavior in the Shiba. Begin early to train your Shiba that aggression toward people over food is an unacceptable behavior. Shortly after giving your Shiba her food, before she is finished eating, take the bowl away. If she looks at you with curiosity showing her normal friendly behavior, pet and praise her and return her food. If, on the other hand, she growls or bares her teeth, a correction is required. In a stern voice tell her *"No."* Wait a few minutes to give her the rest of the food. Again, take the food away. Match your response to her behavior. Repeat this exercise frequently and at various times in her development. She may not show a reaction at sixteen weeks, but at six

Food Bowls

Even an empty food bowl can become a source of conflict. Pick up and remove food bowls after feeding. Fifteen minutes is generally a sufficient time to allow your Shiba to finish eating. Even if food remains in the bowl, remove the food bowl so that it is not a source of conflict between pets.

months she may. If you have been consistently letting her know that you can remove her food at will throughout her development, she may never display food aggression to people.

Food aggression with other animals may be more problematic. Observe the behavior of your pets during feeding time. Some Shibas will display guarding behavior. This means that your Shiba may hover around her food bowl, displaying overt dominance or aggression if your other pets approach. This behavior may be reversed by applying a correction when the behavior is observed. Until you are comfortable that your pets are not going to have a confrontation over food, feed only when you are there and in a position to correct unacceptable behavior. You may find that food aggression between your pets is a serious problem. If this is the case, consider feeding separately. Put your Shiba in a crate during mealtime or feed your pets in different rooms or areas of your home.

KEEPING YOUR SHIBA INU HEALTHY AND WELL GROOMED

Shibas are fundamentally a very healthy and hardy breed. Many Shibas live long, healthy lives, visiting the veterinarian only for routinely scheduled preventive care visits. Grooming is easy, too.

The Shiba is a very stoic dog and in many respects acts like her ancestor the wolf. If your Shiba is visibly ill, don't wait until tomorrow to see if she is feeling better—*go to the veterinarian now.* If you wait until tomorrow, it may be too late. A wild dog or wolf will mask illness as long as she can, to avoid being left behind by the pack. Shibas display many characteristics of primitive or wild dogs. Your Shiba may have been masking symptoms of illness and now her condition is an emergency.

Working with Your Veterinarian

Responsible dog ownership is often a series of partnerships. Raising a Shiba puppy to become a healthy, well-adjusted adult that others enjoy being around is a challenge that is often overcome with three or four important partnerships. Your responsible breeder is one important partnership and is a strong support system for help and guidance. Your trainer or handler is another important partnership. He or she will work with you and your family to assist with any problem behavior and to work with you in a joint effort to raise a well-behaved adult. Your dog groomer, if you select a professional, will also provide you with a wealth of information and advice. All of these partnerships are important, but perhaps the most important partnership in a long, healthy, and satisfying life for your dog, is the partnership you form with your veterinarian.

Remember when you are interviewing veterinarians that you are forming a partnership where finding the right veterinarian can prove difficult. While the Shiba is not a special needs breed for major or common health issues, it can be a special needs breed for behavioral issues. Many veterinarians express wariness at having Shibas as clients. Some bad-mannered and badly trained Shibas have helped to establish the Shiba's undeserved reputation as a feral, aggressive, and vicious breed. It is important that your veterinarian is comfortable working with the breed and that his or her approach to your dog is done with confidence.

The Shiba is a master of intimidation. If your veterinarian approaches your puppy to give her a vaccination and she growls, the worst thing that can happen is for your veterinarian to retreat or act startled—the little bully will have won a battle of wills, and an inappropriate message is sent to the Shiba. Anytime a puppy shows any sign of aggressive behavior, you must act immediately. Determine if you are observing dominance or fear aggression. Fear aggression is met with reassurance. Calm your Shiba with gentle handling and a voice cue that signals that the situation is not threatening. When your Shiba is assured, continue with the activity. Dominance aggression is met with a stern correction, signaling that she is not in control—you are. Your Shiba puppy needs to learn her place in the hierarchy: *below all humans.* A confident veterinarian will not adversely react to the puppy's inappropriate behavior; instead, he or she will firmly, but gently, impose his or her will on the puppy.

During the first year of her life, your Shiba will visit the veterinarian frequently, completing her vaccination and deworming schedule. This is an important time for your Shiba and veterinarian to build rapport. This relationship may be important later on in your Shiba's life if she requires emergency care.

CHECKLIST

Veterinary Care
✔ Record your veterinarian contact and emergency numbers.
✔ Create a first aid kit for your Shiba.
✔ Establish and follow an immunization schedule.
✔ Establish and follow a deworming schedule, including year-round heartworm preventive.
✔ Establish a plan for the control of external parasites.
✔ Discuss spaying or neutering your Shiba and plan the best time for you and your Shiba.

Preventive Maintenance

Immunizations
Young puppies are vulnerable to contagious canine viruses. For this reason, many breeders will not allow visitors to play with young puppies, prior to the puppies receiving their first immunization. Many breeders will restrict travel only to the veterinarian in the first eight weeks. It is important to understand when you bring your puppy home that even if she has had one or more inoculations, she does not have immunity to many of the contagious canine viruses. A complete series of inoculations is required before your Shiba has built immunity. Please restrict your puppy's travel in areas with heavy dog traffic until after the series is complete. Dog parks and visits to the

pet store can provide important and necessary socialization experiences, but you should wait until the vaccination cycle is complete before allowing your puppy free access to these types of locations.

When the puppy reaches eight weeks, she should have had her first immunization. The first immunization in the puppy series should include at a minimum: canine distemper, parainfluenza, adenovirus type 2, and parvovirus. Many breeders and veterinarians choose to wait until the puppy is older to administer immunizations for rabies, coronavirus, and bordatella. Some breeders and veterinarians do not recommend immunization for Lyme disease and leptospira bacterin. Prior to having these immunizations, discuss with the breeder and veterinarian any regulatory requirements and any potential adverse reactions, as well as the risk of contracting the disease in your region of the country.

Provide your veterinarian with your puppy's shot record. You will have received this from your breeder. Your veterinarian may have a set schedule he or she prefers and you may safely follow his or her schedule. One important piece of information to remember is that some breeders have experienced Shibas becoming infected with canine parvovirus after the Shiba was thought to be fully immunized. For this reason, many breeders recommend an additional vaccine in the parvovirus series, administered after the puppy is 20 weeks old. Listed is an immunization schedule Shiba breeders have found effective, which you may wish to consider implementing.

Parasite Control

If you are going to own a dog, you are going to deal with parasites. The canine is host to a

Suggested Immunization Schedule

Age	Immunization
8 weeks	DA$_2$PP
10 weeks	
12 weeks	DA$_2$PP
12 weeks	*Rabies (1 year vaccine)
	**Bordatella
	**Coronavirus
	**Lyme disease
	**Leptospira bacterin
16 weeks	DA$_2$PP
16 weeks	***Lyme booster
	***Bordatella booster
	***Leptospira bacteria booster
16 weeks	Coronavirus
20 weeks	Parvovirus

*Many veterinarians and breeders prefer to wait until the puppy is older to administer the rabies vaccination. Rabies vaccination is regulated in many regions. Follow the advice of your veterinarian to assure you are within compliance of local laws and requirements.
**If determined desirable after discussion with the breeder and veterinarian.
***If given at twelve weeks.

wide array of parasites, from a variety of worms to fleas and ticks. Keeping your Shiba parasite-free is important to the overall health of your dog. Breeders begin a regular deworming schedule while the puppies are young and should supply new owners with a copy of the schedule and a recommendation for controlling internal parasites. The internal parasite cycle will require multiple deworming treatments to break the cycle. This process will continue until the puppy is approximately twelve weeks of age, at which time your puppy should begin year-round heartworm preventive medication. The breeder should also supply new owners with recommendations for the control of external parasites, such as fleas and ticks. It is often beneficial to bring in a fecal sample for your first veterinary visit. Your veterinarian will recommend a deworming schedule, as well as supplying recommendations for year-round heartworm preventive and flea and tick control. One piece of information to consider is that a new method of preventing heartworm infestation has been introduced. This is a shot the dog receives every six months, instead of an oral application. This is a new treatment and the results are not well published; however, some Shibas have experienced a violent allergic reaction to this type of heartworm control. Until further studies are complete, it is advisable to use the well-established oral preventative.

Spaying or Neutering

Most of the gender differences develop through the maturation process, and hormonal development triggers many distinctive characteristics, as well as problematic behavior. Spaying or neutering the puppy at a young age minimizes the tendency toward dog aggression and the gender differences developed hormonally through the growth cycle.

If you do not plan to actively participate in the sport of purebred dogs or to become active as a breeder, spaying or neutering your Shiba prior to the completion of sexual maturity will provide a delightful companion and minimize many of the negative gender or hormonal characteristics and behaviors. Neutered males may not develop marking behaviors, will have a reduced tendency toward dog aggression, and will most likely display more patience with young children. Spayed females will not display the seasonal aggression toward dogs and/or people tied to the reproductive process and the instinct to protect their young. Additionally, you will not have to deal with the inconvenience of a female in estrus, such as vaginal bleeding, vaginal discharge, and unwanted visits from intact males in your neighborhood.

While no surgical procedure is without risk, the benefits associated with surgically altering your Shiba's reproductive system far outweigh the risks. Advances in veterinary medicine have found that spaying or neutering too young has the potential to create unintended side effects. There are studies that seem to support the introduction or escalation of aggressive behavior in females spayed prior to their first estrus cycle. There are also studies that suggest that males neutered at a very young age do not reach full physical maturity in comparison

═CHECKLIST═

Spaying and Neutering Myths
✔ Spaying or neutering reduces food intake, promoting weight loss.
✔ Spaying or neutering increases food intake, promoting weight gain and obesity.
✔ Spaying or neutering reduces growth rate or stunts growth.
✔ Spaying or neutering creates depression and affects the dog's mental well-being.

with males of the same breed and lineage that remain intact. Please discuss the potential benefits and side effects with your veterinarian to determine the best age to spay or neuter your Shiba. Some of the benefits of spaying or neutering your Shiba at a relatively young age include:

• Reduces the risk of breast or mammary cancer if the ovaries are removed.
• Prevents testicular, uterine, and ovarian diseases and infections.
• Prevents unwanted pregnancies.
• Allows rapid recovery and healing time
• Young dogs recover quickly from surgical procedures.

Common Health Problems in the Shiba Inu

Health issues that occur frequently and are pervasive with the Shiba Inu are: allergies, chronic circling, cancer, disorders of the eye, hip dysplasia, hock luxation, patellar luxation, and vestibular disorder.

Allergies

Allergic reactions to several stimulants have been reported. Common sources for allergies are food, grass, mold, trees, pollen, and other environmental stimulants. Severe reactions have been reported to vaccines, insect stings, snake bites, and anesthesia. Some Shibas develop allergies later in life that frequently manifest as skin disorders. The irritation will cause frequent scratching resulting in bald patches. If your Shiba is scratching to the extent that bald patches of this type occur, please contact your veterinarian. It may be impossible or impractical to remove the allergic stimulant from the environment. In this situation, your veterinarian may provide a prescription medication to reduce or eliminate the allergic response. If the medication resolves the irritation, it is not uncommon for the Shiba to take this medication for the rest of her life.

Chronic Circling or Spinning

The Shiba continuously runs in a circle or spins. Frequently, an affected dog will only spin in one direction, i.e. clockwise, but is able to turn in the other direction if a barrier is provided. These Shibas are often able to focus on tasks without circling, however, during stress or excitement, the Shiba will start circling. For example, if they have to relieve themselves or if they are excited to see someone, Shibas will start running in a circle. The frequency of circling often increases when the Shiba is confined to a run or a crate.

Spinning can be moderate or severe. A dog who occasionally circles is not a spinner. A true spinner is unmistakable. It is not an occasional behavior—it is marked by a clear pattern. Several breeders have theories as to the physiological source. Potential culprits include: neurological disorders, behavioral disorders, inner ear problems, dietary deficiencies, and a form of epilepsy. Studies are being conducted in other breeds exhibiting similar behavior. Shiba breeders are hopeful these studies will produce results that will prove insightful to this common problem.

Cancer

A variety of cancer associated diseases occur in all canines. The National Canine Cancer Foundation reports that one in three dogs will develop some form of cancer. The good news for Shiba owners is that the reported cases of cancer in the Shiba are well below the average across all canine species. A variety of cancers in Shibas have been reported, however, these reports are infrequent compared to other health related issues.

Eye Disorders

There are several disorders of the eye that occur in Shibas. It is still too early in breed history to provide any estimation of frequency of occurrence. It is hopeful that in time, with an accurate and well documented CERF data base, breeders will understand the likelihood of occurrence. At the present time, screening the Shiba's parents is the only viable option. Scientists have discovered the genetic markers for certain eye diseases in some breeds and an evaluation of the dogs DNA provides valuable information. However, this type of information is not available for the Shiba at this time. The eye disorders reported are:

Cataracts: Early onset or juvenile cataracts are diagnosed in relation to the age of the dog at the time of occurrence. This may lead to

CHECKLIST

Eye Disorders

✔ **Entropion**: A condition where the upper or lower lid turns under or is inverted. Lashes can damage the cornea.

✔ **Ectropion**: A condition where the upper or lower lid turns out or is everted. Lashes can damage the cornea.

✔ **Microphthalmia**: A condition where the eye is abnormally small.

✔ **Glaucoma**: Condition that occurs when the function of the eye is impaird by an elevation of intraocular pressure (IOP).

✔ **Progressive retinal atrophy (PRA):** The name given to a group of hereditary diseases in dogs that affect the retina. The various classifications of the disease are determined by the specific pathology and the age of onset. Complete blindness occurs with almost all forms of PRA. Night blindness is frequently the first noticeable symptom of PRA. Often, pupils are dilated and the back of the eye appears shiny. PRA is an autosomal recessive gene.

✔ **Juvenile cataracts**: The appearance of cataracts in unusually young dogs. This may lead to blindness or the cataract may remain small and not interfere with vision.

blindness or the cataract may remain small and not interfere with vision. Late onset cataracts are also diagnosed in relation to the dog's age, frequently occurring late in the senior dog's life. Most research is conducted with regard to the occurrence of juvenile cataracts where an

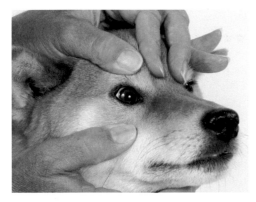

otherwise healthy dog loses sight between the ages of two and six years old.

Entropion: A condition where the upper or lower lid turns under or is inverted. Lashes can damage the cornea.

Ectropion: A condition where the upper or lower lid turns out or is everted. Lashes can damage the cornea.

Microphthalmia: The condition where the eye is abnormally small.

Glaucoma: Glaucoma occurs when the function of the eye is impaired by an elevation of intraocular pressure (IOP).

Progressive retinal atrophy: Progressive retinal atrophy (PRA) is the name given to a group of hereditary diseases in dogs that affect the retina. The various classifications of the disease are determined by the specific pathology and the age of onset. Complete blindness occurs with almost all forms of PRA. Night blindness is frequently the first noticeable symptom of PRA. Often, pupils are dilated and the back of the eye appears shiny. PRA is an autosomal recessive gene.

The eye disorders reported with the highest frequency are glaucoma, entropion, and cataracts. Among the instances of cataracts diagnosed in young Shibas, most are classified as punctate or seed cataracts, where the dog's vision is not impaired and the significance of these are classified as unknown.

Hip Dysplasia

While the percentage of Shibas diagnosed with hip dysplasia is not reliable at this point in breed history, there have been Shibas diagnosed with hip dysplasia. Young adults can be screened for hip dysplasia using two accepted techniques.

⏤⏤(HE(KLIST⏤⏤

First Aid Emergency Kit
- ✔ Milk of magnesia for constipation
- ✔ Kaopectate for diarrhea
- ✔ Neosporin for topical application to abrasions, wounds, and cuts
- ✔ Ipecac syrup to induce vomiting
- ✔ Hydrogen peroxide 3% solution to induce vomiting and clean abrasions, wounds, and cuts
- ✔ Betadine solution to disinfect abrasions, wounds, and cuts
- ✔ Sterile saline solution to flush eyes or abrasions, wounds, and cuts
- ✔ Activated charcoal in case of poisioning
- ✔ Flashlight
- ✔ Tweezers
- ✔ Thermometer
- ✔ Tourniquet
- ✔ Cotton balls
- ✔ Q-tips
- ✔ Gauze pads
- ✔ Paper towels

Both OFA and Penn Hip employ programs that diagnose this problem and registries to record the results. Breeders frequently have one or more of these tests performed prior to breeding. While parents with clear hips are not a guarantee that a puppy will not have hip dysplasia as an adult, there is data supporting a genetic correlation to canine hip dysplasia. If the parents are clear, the chance of a puppy developing the disease is reduced. A Shiba with hip dysplasia will generally not manifest symptoms in the same manner as a larger breed, due mostly to the weight burden on the joints. Some Shibas with hip dysplasia are never symptomatic for the disease until very late in life.

Patellar Luxation

This condition occurs when the patella (kneecap) does not seat firmly—the kneecap moves out of place and may require surgery to repair the condition. The Orthopedic Foundation for Animals (OFA) has created the following scale for patellar luxation.

Patellar Luxation

This condition occurs when the patella (kneecap) does not seat firmly—the kneecap moves out of place and may require surgery to repair the condition. The Orthopedic Foundation for Animals (OFA) has created the following scale for patellar luxation.

Grade	Description	Treatment
Grade 1	Patella is able to be moved with manual palpation, however dog is not symptomatic.	Surgery not recommended
Grade 2	Patella slips occasionally, but moves back into place.	Surgery not recommended
Grade 3	Patella slips frequently, but moves back into place.	Surgery may be required
Grade 4	Patella is out of place; will not get back into position.	Surgery required

Peripheral Vestibular Syndrome

This disorder or syndrome is frequently confused with a stroke and most often occurs in geriatric dogs, but can appear in middle aged dogs as well. It typically has a sudden onset where the dog is unable to stand or appears disoriented. This condition lasts between two days and up to three weeks, after which the dog typically recovers without any residual effects. However, in some cases, the dog will have a head tilt after recovery. This is thought to be the result of inflammation of the nerves between the inner ear and the cerebellum, the portion of the brain that controls balance and spatial orientation. After onset of the syndrome, the dog will typically refrain from eating or drinking. Hand feeding and watering the dog is required to provide support care until the dog returns to normal and is able to stand and move again.

The Senior Shiba Inu

As your Shiba matures she will experience the typical effects of aging. As the color on her face fades to white, her activity level will

decrease; however, your Shiba may act like a puppy well into her senior years. Work with your veterinarian to determine any specific requirements for your aging Shiba. Check blood levels more frequently, as this is often an early indicator of health problems that if diagnosed early may be treated instead of proving fatal.

Euthanasia

Making the decision to say good-bye to a well-loved friend is never easy. However, balancing the quality of life versus painful treatments or extended suffering for a condition without treatment is a decision you may be faced with at some point. If you find yourself asking if it is time, you may want to have a discussion with your veterinarian, who will be able to help you put the known facts into prospective. You may have a hard time balancing your Shiba's needs against your own. This is not uncommon because our Shibas give us so much and are such an important part of our life.

If you and your veterinarian have come to the decision that euthanasia is the right choice for your Shiba, schedule an appointment. Discuss the situation with family members and make sure everyone has a chance to say good-bye. Some family members may want to be present to comfort your Shiba during the procedure; other members may choose not to participate. This should be an individual choice, with the exception of young children. Parents will need to make the decision for the child, considering the child's personality.

Remember that you are considering your Shiba's needs above your own. Allow yourself and your family time to grieve. Don't dwell

on your decision; instead, celebrate the wonderful years you had with your Shiba companion.

Basic Coat Care

Maintaining a healthy, shiny, and thick coat involves three factors: genetics, diet, and grooming. The texture and density of the Shiba coat is largely a function of genetics. Coarse thick guard coats come from your Shiba's parents, not from a bottle of vitamins or shampoo. The correct Shiba coat is a difficult trait to breed and maintain in a breeding program. If your Shiba does not carry a coat like that of

the Shibas you see in books or on televised dog shows, you are not doing something wrong. Don't spend a fortune on costly shampoos or vitamin supplements trying to create a coat your Shiba did not inherit.

Having said that, the condition of the coat your Shiba does have can be influenced by her diet and the materials you use to groom. A healthy, well-balanced diet will create a coat with luster and shine. Grooming your dog regularly will also keep her coat clean and shiny.

Nails

Your Shiba can be very sensitive about her feet. Start with your puppy when she is very young, teaching her to allow her feet to be handled. Her nails should be clipped weekly, barely removing the tips, to get her accustomed to the process and without causing her discomfort. Hold her leg by the elbow to steady it rather than by the pastern or foot. She will object less, saving stress on your eardrums and protecting you from scratches during a struggle. You may wish to wear a thick shirt with long sleeves and long pants to protect your arms and legs from scratches during grooming.

Nail trimming is one of the activities that can elicit the "Shiba Scream" and is a frequent source of this high drama. The Shiba will often start the scream merely at the site of the clippers or grinder. If you are where others can hear, they will come running to you and your Shiba, firmly convinced that your Shiba is mortally wounded. Imagine the surprise when they find your Shiba without a scratch.

Shibas also have long memories. You may have trimmed her nails many times without

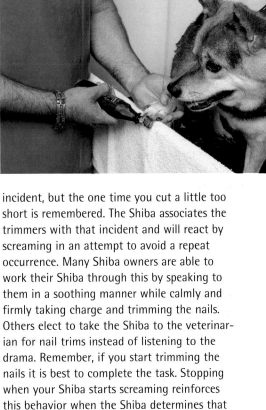

incident, but the one time you cut a little too short is remembered. The Shiba associates the trimmers with that incident and will react by screaming in an attempt to avoid a repeat occurrence. Many Shiba owners are able to work their Shiba through this by speaking to them in a soothing manner while calmly and firmly taking charge and trimming the nails. Others elect to take the Shiba to the veterinarian for nail trims instead of listening to the drama. Remember, if you start trimming the nails it is best to complete the task. Stopping when your Shiba starts screaming reinforces this behavior when the Shiba determines that you will stop the activity if they scream.

The Shiba Inu is known as a "wash-and-wear" dog because she requires so little grooming. Every dog, however, does require a certain amount of grooming for the health and well-being of her skin and coat.

Bathing

Unless she has gotten into something that makes her really smelly or muddy, the Shiba shouldn't require more than one bath per month. At a minimum, the Shiba should be bathed twice a year during her shedding season to help remove the dead coat. A mild shampoo that will not soften the coat should be applied liberally into a wet coat. Work the shampoo into lather, paying particular attention to legs, feet, and underside. Rinse with warm water until water runs absolutely clear. If shampoo isn't completely removed, it may cause the skin to become dry and flaky, which, in turn, causes the dog to scratch and possibly create hot spots (inflamed red areas that may become infected). If the dog is particularly dirty, the shampoo may be repeated; otherwise, one shampoo is usually sufficient.

Drying

If this is a routine shampoo and weather permits, your Shiba may be vigorously tow-

eled and allowed to air dry. If you are preparing the dog for a show or if the weather is cold, she should be blown dry with a dryer that does not contain a heat element. If you are unable to locate a dryer that does not contain a heat element, you may use a traditional blow dryer on the lowest heat setting. If you use a dryer with a heat element, you may wish to take frequent breaks during the drying process. Blow the coat against the grain so that it stands away from the body. Never blow or brush the coat so that it lays flat. Special attention should be paid to the legs and feet, to also be sure that the hair in these areas stands out.

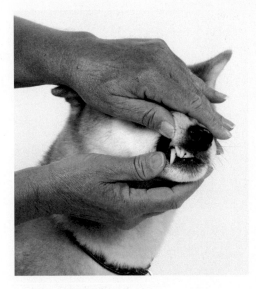

Teeth

Teach your puppy to have her teeth brushed weekly with a commercial doggie toothbrush and paste. This will save veterinary bills later in her life in order to keep her teeth clean. Check the molars and scrape with a flat-edged tooth scaler, if necessary. Feeding a dry food and supplying her with chew toys and bones will aid in keeping her teeth and gums clean and healthy.

Maintaining the Transitional Coat

The Shiba has a double coat with two distinct types of fur. One type of hair is the coarse and harsh guard coat, the other is the soft and dense undercoat. The typical Shiba sheds her undercoat twice a year. This hair comes out in clumps, with the shedding process lasting between three and four weeks. After your Shiba has shed her coat, she will look like a different dog.

A common mistake Shiba owners make is to equate the loss of undercoat with weight loss. Because your Shiba looks smaller after shedding her coat, it's easy to assume she has lost weight. If you increase your Shiba's food intake to compensate, in a month or two, when her new coat grows, it will be obvious she has become overweight.

Shedding her coat is a natural process for the Shiba, and is of a relatively short duration. However, occasionally, the transition between the puppy and adult coat can take longer than the typical shedding experience. Don't become alarmed if your adolescent Shiba is out of coat for as long as six months. When your Shiba loses her undercoat, she will shed her coat everywhere; however, with proper grooming, the amount of fur you remove from carpets and upholstery is minimized.

Begin with a warm bath. After bathing, much of the loose undercoat can be removed by brushing and combing. Removing Shiba coat during the shedding season can be tedious. The best way to accomplish it is to brush the hair with a slicker brush, against the grain. With a medium- to fine-toothed metal comb, comb out the dead coat in one-inch sections. Carefully comb each one-inch section until no more undercoat comes out. Removing the dead undercoat in this manner will keep it from shedding all over your house and furniture.

ACTIVITIES FOR YOUR SHIBA INU

Your Shiba is hardy and versatile and will enjoy a wide variety of activities. While some are content to curl up on the couch, the vast majority are active, energetic, and curious, enjoying many forms of physical activity.

Before you try out a new sport or activity with your Shiba, make sure the level of training she has received matches the activity. In other words, if your Shiba reliably comes to you when you call her name, allowing her to swim in a lake or pond where she can exit the water at various points, is an example of matching the training level to the activity.

Hunting

The Shiba was bred to hunt and her instincts are still very strong. Hunting as a sport has decreased in popularity; however, if this is a sport you enjoy, your Shiba will be a willing participant. The Shiba will flush or track game and is not used as a pointer. In Japan, Nippo holds a national boar hunt once a year and three regional boar hunts where Shibas may participate. In the United States, the AKC does not recognize the Shiba as a hunting breed, and Shibas are not eligible for competitive field trials. However, many individuals enjoy hunting with their Shibas mainly for birds and small game.

Conformation Dog Shows

Today, Shibas routinely compete at most conformation dog shows around the globe. While Shibas exhibit in hundreds of All Breed competitions during a year, there are three sets of events specifically created to showcase the Shiba Inu.

Nippo Shows Held in Japan

Nippo supports and holds several regional conformation events during the spring and fall seasons, culminating in the prestigious Grand National, held every November. Shibas must qualify at a regional show to receive an invitation to participate at the Grand National and every year about 700 Shibas exhibit at this event. Nippo celebrated the 100th Grand National in November 2003.

Other Nippo Events

Nippo supports Shiba clubs around the globe, by sending judges to officiate at Nippo events outside of Japan. Two of these events are the Colonial Shiba Club's Nippo Classic and the Beikokou Shiba Inu Aikokai (BSA) show. The Colonial Shiba Club hosts the "Nippo Classic" the third weekend in May at a rotating location on the U.S. East Coast. This event brings a Nippo judge from Japan to host a symposium where participants learn about the Japanese dog in the country of origin. The Colonial Shiba Club allows all native Japanese dogs to

participate and the two-day event brings dogs from all over the United States and Canada where 50 to 75 Shibas, along with other native Japanese breeds, compete for the coveted Nippo USA Championship. BSA hosts a similar show in California in March. The BSA rules allow only Nippo-registered and -owned Shibas to compete at this event. Due to these entry restrictions there are fewer participants (about 25), but the competition is fierce for the privilege of winning the top honors.

AKC- and NSCA-Sponsored National and Regional Specialty Shows

Once a year, the NSCA sponsors its National Specialty show. This show rotates locations, moving to a different part of the United States each year. The numbers of participants vary, due to the demographics of the region, but the show has a standard format offering a variety of events and activities spanning a two- to four-day period.

Regional Specialty shows are held each year throughout the United States. Information on these shows is obtained by contacting the NSCA or one of the Regional Shiba Clubs listed in the Information or event section.

Obedience Trials

Shibas participate in AKC-sponsored obedience trials on a regular basis, with several earning CD, CDX, and UD titles. While, it takes a lot of training and preparation to compete in obedience trials with a Shiba, competing with a well-trained Shiba is a fun and rewarding experience. Obedience trials offer three levels of competition: Novice, Open, and Utility. The participating dog must qualify at three

events, or earn three legs, to earn an obedience title. It may be difficult to earn an obedience title with a Shiba, but Ch Fanfair's Kiwi of Nikima, CD, earned her title in only three shows, qualifying at each competition where she participated, even earning the High in Trial award at one of her All Breed events. Earning a title in three shows is a record that can never be broken, only tied. She made it look easy and showed it can be done!

Rally

The varying nature of the Rally course designed by the judge keeps the Shiba challenged and engaged. The opportunity to work as a team is a favorite with Shibas and owners alike. These competitive events are not as rigorous as an obedience trial and are more forgiving of the Shiba's natural tendency to solve problems and find an optimal method of completing any task.

Agility Trials

Shibas enjoy participating in agility events and perform well at these competitions throughout the United States, with several earning titles. These athletic events provide a variety of obstacles for the Shiba to travel over, under, around, and through. Events are timed, providing a competitive experience that is exciting, fun, and rewarding for both human and canine participants.

Shibas excel in agility and find the challenge of a changing course stimulating. The opportunity to run, play, and surmount multiple obstacles at their owner's side explains the high number of Shibas earning titles each year in competitive agility events.

Canine Good Citizens and Therapy Dog Activities

The AKC Canine Good Citizen (CGC) program recognizes dogs that display good manners in the community as well as at home. This training step is often a good starting point for your Shiba. The program offers a variety of socialization opportunities with both people and other dogs.

Therapy dogs are dogs that make a difference in the lives of others. These dogs enjoy meeting strangers, love children, and enjoy the company of other dogs. Certification is achieved through Therapy Dogs International.

Once certified, the Shiba will spread joy and love with hospice and nursing home residents, children in cancer wards, and anywhere that a wagging tail and a warm greeting creates a bright spot in someone's day. For information on the program visit the TDI web site at *www.tdi-dog.org* or by phone at (973) 252-9800.

Other Activities

Walking

Perhaps the most common activity for the Shiba is taking walks with her owner. The Shiba's curious nature makes her a willing participant on walks with her owner on city streets or country roads.

While strangers may think nothing of approaching you and your Shiba, your Shiba may not appreciate strangers petting, poking, or prodding her. Shibas can also be protective of their owners if they perceive a threat. Biting dogs are not tolerated in today's society; therefore, it is up to you to protect your dog. If your dog appears uncomfortable, excuse yourself and leave. A forced introduction with a stranger when your Shiba is uncomfortable may turn into an unfortunate experience.

Jogging

The athletic Shiba is a delightful jogging companion. She will keep pace with you on long or short runs. There are a few important considerations when jogging with your Shiba. Young puppies are not physically mature for long runs; work up to longer distances as your Shiba ages. A pounding or jarring motion on hard surfaces, such as concrete or asphalt, can be hard or your dog's joints. Run on grass or turf, if possible. Choose your running paths

carefully to avoid high traffic areas, and for night runs wear reflective materials on you and your dog.

Hiking

Shibas enjoy camping and hiking as much as you do. Your Shiba will hike most trails without difficulty. Remember, the Shiba is a hunter. Most wooded areas and hiking trails contain a vast array of prey for your Shiba. The movement of nature's creatures coupled with the exciting new scents will call to her natural instincts. Protect her from herself. Keep your Shiba on a lead for hiking to protect her from becoming lost or injured. This curious hunter will approach snakes, porcupines, and other animals capable of inflicting serious damage, without hesitation.

Swimming

Many Shibas enjoy swimming, boating, and water sports; other Shibas want nothing to do with water. These Shibas seem to associate being wet with being dirty and these clean Shibas will avoid water at all cost. Participation in sports involving water will vary between individuals—either she'll love it or hate it. Training a young Shiba to accept and participate in water sports may prove beneficial, but even then, some Shibas will choose to make any contact with water a struggle.

Fetch

Shibas love a game of catch. Balls are prized possessions and Shibas will play catch tirelessly for hours. Frisbee and flyball are also fetching activities Shibas enjoy. A word of caution is necessary for Shibas participating with Frisbees or flyball: For a period the Shiba is off her leash and instead of returning the ball to you,

she may take the ball and leave to explore the area. Shibas can also be possessive with toys and may decide the ball belongs to her and other dogs are not allowed to play.

Napping

Your active Shiba will typically sleep between 13 to 16 hours each day. Shibas have long periods of sleep as well as frequent short naps. The amount of sleep your Shiba will need in a day will vary depending upon her age and from season to season. At extreme temperature ranges, such as winter and summer, your Shiba will typically require more sleep. Many Shibas adjust their sleeping patterns to match those of their family. After a morning hike together, you may benefit from a short nap and so will your Shiba.

THE AKC STANDARD FOR THE SHIBA INU

Every AKC recognized breed has one National Club. The National Club, the NSCA for the Shiba Inu, is responsible for writing a Standard of Excellence for the breed within the AKC guidelines and making changes to the Standard when the Club members feel a change is needed or desirable. The AKC approves and adopts the Standard, and this Standard becomes the yardstick by which dogs are judged at AKC conformation shows and the ideal that breeders strive toward in their breeding programs.

General Appearance

The Shiba is the smallest of the Japanese native breeds of dog and was originally developed for hunting by sight and scent in the dense undergrowth of Japan's mountainous areas. Alert and agile with keen senses, he is also an excellent watchdog and companion. His frame is compact with well-developed muscles. Males and females are distinctly different in appearance: males are masculine without coarseness, females are feminine without weakness of structure.

Size, Proportion, Substance

Males 14½ inches to 16½ inches at withers. Females 13½ inches to 15½ inches. The pre-ferred size is the middle of the range for each sex. Average weight at preferred size is approximately 23 pounds for males, 17 pounds for females. Males have a height to length ratio of 10 to 11, females slightly longer. Bone is moderate. *Disqualification— Males over 16½ inches and under 14½ inches. Females over 15½ inches and under 13½ inches.*

Head

Expression is good natured with a strong and confident gaze. *Eyes* are somewhat triangular in shape, deep set, and upward slanting toward the outside base of the ear. Iris is dark brown. Eye rims are black. *Ears* are triangular in shape, firmly pricked and small, but in proportion to head and body size. Ears are set well apart and tilt directly forward with the slant of the back of the ear following the arch of the neck. *Skull* size is moderate and in proportion to the body. *Forehead* is broad and flat with a slight furrow. *Stop* is moderate. *Muzzle* is firm, full, and round with a stronger lower jaw projecting from full *cheeks*. The bridge of the muzzle is straight. Muzzle tapers slightly from stop to nose tip. Muzzle length is 40% of the total head length from occiput to nose tip. It is preferred that whiskers remain intact. *Lips* are tight and black. *Nose* is black. *Bite* is scissors, with a full complement of strong, substantial, evenly aligned teeth. *Serious Fault*—Five or more missing teeth is a very serious fault and must be penalized. *Disqualification—Overshot or undershot bite.*

Neck, Topline, and Body

Neck is thick, sturdy, and of moderate length. *Topline* is straight and level to the base of the tail. *Body* is dry and well muscled without the appearance of sluggishness or coarseness. Forechest is well developed. Chest depth measured from the withers to the lowest point of the sternum is one-half or slightly less than the total height from withers to ground. *Ribs* are moderately sprung. *Abdomen* is firm and well tucked-up. *Back* is firm. *Loins* are strong. *Tail* is thick and powerful and is carried over the back in a sickle or curled position. A loose single curl or sickle tail pointing vigorously toward the neck and nearly parallel to the back is preferred. A double curl or sickle tail pointing upward is acceptable. In length the tail reaches nearly to the hock joint when extended. Tail is set high.

Forequarters

Shoulder blade and upper arm are moderately angulated and approximately equal in length. Elbows are set close to the body and turn neither in nor out. Forelegs and feet are moderately spaced, straight, and parallel. Pasterns are slightly inclined. Removal of front dewclaws is optional. Feet are catlike with well-arched toes fitting tightly together. Pads are thick.

Hindquarters

The angulation of the hindquarters is moderate and in balance with the angulation of the forequarters. Hind legs are strong with a wide natural stance. The hock joint is strong, turning neither in nor out. Upper thighs are long and the second thighs short but well developed. No dewclaws. Feet as in forequarters.

Coat

Double coated with the outer coat being stiff and straight and the undercoat soft and thick. Fur is short and even on face, ears, and legs. Guard hairs stand off the body and are about 1½ to 2 inches in length at the withers. Tail hair is slightly longer and stands open in a brush. It is preferred that the Shiba be presented in a natural state. *Trimming of the coat must be severely penalized. Serious Fault—*Long or woolly coat.

Color

Coat color is as specified herein, with the three allowed colors given equal consideration. All colors are clear and intense. The undercoat is cream, buff, or gray. *Urajiro* (cream to white ventral color) is required in the following areas on all coat colors: on the sides of the muzzle, on the cheeks, inside the ears, on the underjaw and upper throat, inside of legs, on the abdomen, around the vent and the ventral side of the tail. On *reds:* commonly on the throat, forechest, and chest. On *blacks and sesames:* commonly as a triangular mark on both sides of the forechest. White spots above the eyes permitted on all colors but not required. Bright orange-red with urajiro lending a foxlike appearance to dogs of this color. Clear red preferred but a very slight dash of black tipping is permitted on the back and tail. *Black with tan points* and ura-jiro. Black hairs have a brownish cast, not blue. The undercoat is buff or gray. The borderline between black and tan areas is clearly defined. Tan points are located as follows: two oval spots over the eyes: on the sides of the muzzle between the black bridge of the muzzle and the white cheeks; on the outside of the forelegs from the carpus, or a little above, downward to the toes; on the outside of the hind legs down the front of the stifle broadening from hock joint to toes, but not completely eliminating black from rear of pasterns. Black penciling on toes permitted. Tan hairs may also be found on the inside of the ear and on the underside of the tail. Sesame (black-tipped hairs on a rich red background) with urajiro. Tipping is light and even on the body and head with no concentration of black in any area. Sesame areas appear at least one-half red. Sesame may end in a widow's peak on the forehead, leaving the bridge and sides of the muzzle red. Eye spots and lower legs are also red. Clearly delineated white markings are permitted but not required on the tip of the tail and in the form of socks on the forelegs to the elbow joint, hind legs to the knee joint. A patch of blaze is permitted on the throat, forechest, or chest in addition to urajiro. *Serious fault*—Cream, white pinto, or any other color or marking not specified is a very serious fault and must be penalized.

Gait

Movement is nimble, light, and elastic. At the trot, the legs angle in toward a center line while the topline remains level and firm. Forward reach and rear extension are moderate and efficient. In the show ring, the Shiba is gaited on a loose lead at a brisk trot.

Temperament

A spirited boldness, a good nature, and an unaffected forthrightness, which together yield dignity and natural beauty. The Shiba has an independent nature and can be reserved toward strangers but is loyal and affectionate to those who earn his respect. At times aggressive toward other dogs, the Shiba is always under the control of his handler. Any aggression toward handler or judge or any overt shyness must be severely penalized.

Summary

The foregoing is a description of the ideal Shiba. Any deviation from the above standard is to be considered a fault and must be penalized. The severity of the fault is equal to the extent of the deviation. A harmonious balance of form, color, movement, and temperament is more critical than any one feature.

Disqualifications

Males over 16½ and under 14½ inches.
Females over 15½ and under 13½ inches.
Overshot or undershot bite.

INFORMATION

Registries for the Shiba Inu

The American Kennel Club (AKC)
5580 Centerview Drive
Raleigh, NC 27606
(919) 233-9767

The Canadian Kennel Club
89 Skyway Avenue, Suite 100
Etobicoke, Ontario, Canada M9W 6R4
(416) 675-5511

Federation Cynologique Internationale
Secretariat General de la FCA
Place Albert 1er, 13
B-6530 Thuin, Belgium
www.fci.be/english

Japan Kennel Club (JKC)
1-5 Kanda, Chiyoda-ku
Tokyo, 101 Japan

The Kennel Club
1-4 Clargis Street, Picadilly
London W7Y 8AB England

Nihonken Hozonkai (Nippo)
Surugadai Sanraizu Bldg. 1F
2-11-1 Kanda, Surugadai
Chiyoda-ku, Tokyo 101-0062 Japan

Purebred Dog and Shiba Specialty Clubs

The American Kennel Club
5580 Centerview Drive
Raleigh, NC 27606
(919) 233-9767

National Shiba Club of America

Contact information changes yearly and
current information is available on the club
website. *www.shibas.org*

Arizona Shiba Inu Association

Wendy Bonville
8509 W. Sheridan Street
Phoenix, AZ 85037
(623) 849-5281
asahishibas@podigy.net

Beikoku Shiba Inu Aikokai (BSA)

Kai Katsumoto
2842 Elmlawn Drive
Anaheim, CA 92804
(714) 821-9218

Blue & Gray Shiba Fanciers

Maggi Strouse
3357 Glen Eden Quay
Virginia Beach, VA 23452
(757) 618-0505
fairwyn@verizon.net

Colonial Shiba Club

Laura Payton
PO Box 346
Jamestown, KY 42629
(270) 866-9275
fanfair@aol.com

Evergreen Shiba Inu Club

Website: *www.evergreenshibaclub.org*
Dee Van Arnam
2510 Tudor Way S E
Albany, OR 97322
(541) 791-5324
raiderdouglas@msn.com

Great Lakes Shiba Fanciers
Lynea Roszczewski
21010 Pratt Road
Armada, MI 48005
(586) 784-4393
regalshibas@yahoo.com

Heart of Dixie Shiba Fanciers
Kris Johnson
201 Ivy Lakes Drive
St. Johns, FL 32259
(904) 230-2402
krisakita@bellsouth.net

Mid-States Shiba Club
Betty Rarick
2250 South 66th Place West
Muskogee, OK 74401
(918) 683-4297
mss_club@yahoo.com

Shiba Club of Greater New York
Christine Edwards
921 Sugar Hollow Road Apt 2
Tunkhannock, PA 18657
(570) 996-5077

Shiba Club of Southern California
Sally Kim
secretary.scsc@gmail.com

Shiba Inu Fanciers of Northern California
Dorothy Warren
PO Box 2639
Saratoga, CA 95070-2639
(408) 867-2467
dorothy@ranchlake.com
Website: *www.sfnc.org*

National Shiba Club of America Past Presidents
Past Presidents of NSCA still active in the breed.

Leslie Ann Engen
11507 243rd Avenue NE
Redmond, WA 98053
(425) 788-5454
laegen@aol.com

Jacey Holden
3991 W. Peltier Road
Lodi, CA 95242
(209) 369-3473
jholden@jps.net

Laura Payton
PO Box 346
Jamestown, KY 42629
(270) 866-9275
fanfair@aol.com

Lori Pendergast
1903 Country Club Dr.
Dodge City, KS 67801
(620) 225-1876
Pendragon0392@scglobal.net

Mark Peterson
1791 Furnas Road
Vandalia, OH 45377
(614) 332-2446
woofmdp@yahoo.com

Lisa Shery
29272 San Fransquito Canyon Road
Santa Clarita, CA 91390
(310) 367-1503
lisa@sheryblossom.com

Ken Tracy
10864 Peola Road
Clarkston, WA 99403
(509) 751-1088
sanshoushibas@printime.net

Rescue Organizations and Contacts
National
Shiba Inu Rescue Resources of America—
   SIRRA
Website: *national.shibarescue.org/*

Regional
Mid Atlantic Shiba Rescue
Website: *www.midatlanticshibarescue.org*
Serving MD, VA, DC, and S. PA
E-mail: shibarescue.masr@yahoo.com

Midwest Shiba Inu Rescue
A 501-C3 Non-Profit Corporation
Website: *shibarescue.org*
Illinois, Indiana, Michigan, Wisconsin,
Iowa, Minnesota, Kansas, and Missouri
630-225-5046 fax/phone
E-mail: adoptions@shibarescue.org

Northern California Shiba Inu Rescue
Red Young
San Jose, California
E-mail: ShibaK9@aol.com

Northern Nevada Shiba Rescue
Website: *www.myshibainu.com/*
Jack Owens
Reno, Nevada
E-mail: my3shibas@gmail.com

Northwest Shiba Rescue
A 501-C3 Non-Profit Corporation
Website: *www.shibas4life.us*
Serving Oregon & Washington
Denise Roelke
E-mail: shibas4life@gmail.com

NYC Shiba Rescue Inc.
A 501-C3 Non-Profit Corporation
Website: *nycshibarescue.org*
Serving NY, NJ, northern PA, CT, MA and
   surrounding areas
Phone: 917-591-3408
Fax: 212-658-9657
E-mail: shibas@nycshibarescue.org

Saving Shibas Inc.
A 501-C3 Non-Profit Corporation
Website: *www.savingshibasinc.org*
Serving Southern California and surrounding
   areas
E-mail: saveshibas@gmail.com
Facebook: *facebook.com/SavingShibasInc*

Shiba Inu Rescue of Texas Inc.
A 501-C3 Non-Profit Corporation
Website: *www.sirtx.org*
Bryan and Francine Walker
Austin, Texas
E-mail: shibarescue@survivorsoft.com

Tri-State Shiba Inu Rescue, Inc.
A 501-C3 Non-Profit Corporation
Website: *www.tristateshiba.org/*
Serving Ohio, Indiana, and Kentucky and
   surrounding areas
Phone: (513) 876-2864
E-mail: info@tristateshiba.org

Breeder Referral

National Shiba Club of America
www.shibas.org

Publications

Books

The Total Shiba
Gretchen Haskett and Susan Houser
Alpine Publications
225 S. Madison Avenue
Loveland, CO 80537
(800) 777-7257

The Complete Shiba
Maureen Atkinson
Copyright 1998 by Ringpress Books
P.O. Box 8, Lydney
Gloucestershire GL15 6YD, United Kingdom

Howell Book House
A Simon & Schuster/Macmillan Company
1633 Broadway
New York, NY 10019

Magazines

The Shiba E-News
Official publication of
the National Shiba
Club of America
www.shibas.org

Important Note

This pet owner's manual tells the reader how to buy and care for a Shiba Inu. The author and publisher consider it important to point out that the advice given in this book is meant primarily for normally developed puppies from a good breeder—that is, dogs of excellent physical health and good character.

Anyone who adopts a fully grown dog should be aware that the animal has already formed its basic impressions of human beings. The new owner should watch the animal carefully, including its behavior toward humans, and should meet the previous owner. If the dog comes from a shelter, it may be possible to get some information on its background and peculiarities there. There are dogs that, as a result of bad experiences with humans, behave in an unnatural manner or may even bite. Only people that have experience with dogs should take in such an animal.

Caution is further advised in the association of children with dogs, in meetings with other dogs, and in exercising the dog without a leash.

Even well-behaved and carefully supervised dogs sometimes cause damage to someone else's property or cause accidents. It is, therefore, in the owner's interest to be adequately insured against such eventualities, and we strongly urge all dog owners to purchase liability policies that cover their dogs.

I N D E X

About the Author

Laura Payton is a dedicated breeder of the Shiba Inu. When she is not working with her own dogs, she dedicates her time to the NSCA, serving in the past as its President. She is also Secretary/Treasurer of the Blue and Gray Shiba Fanciers, President of the Heart of Dixie Shiba Fanciers, and Board Member of Great Lakes Shiba Fanciers. As President of the Colonial Shiba Club, she is dedicated to maintaining a strong relationship with Nippo and working with the Japanese breeders and judges of the Shiba Inu.

Photo Credits

Seth Casteel: pages 12, 28, 36, 37, 50; Dreamstime: pages 45, 49; iStockphoto: pages 43, 54, 70, 74, 75; Daniel Johnson: pages 5, 48, 52, 55, 60, 61, 73, 79; Shutterstock: pages 2–3, 6, 11, 13, 14, 15, 17, 24, 29, 32, 33, 34, 35, 38, 39, 40, 41, 42, 44, 53, 57, 66, 81, 83, 93; Connie Summers: page 84; Joan Hustace Walker: pages 4, 8, 10, 16, 19, 22, 25, 26, 30, 31, 46, 47, 53, 56, 58, 65, 67, 76, 77, 78 (top and bottom), 80, 82, 85, 86, 87; Angie Wojciechowska: pages 9, 51.

Cover Photos

Joan Hustace Walker: front cover; Angie Wojciechowska: inside front cover; Shutterstock: back cover; Connie Summers: inside back cover.

A Note on Pronouns

Many dog lovers feel that the pronoun "it" is not appropriate when referring to a beloved pet. For this reason, Shiba Inus are referred to as "she" throughout this book unless the topic specifically relates to male dogs. No gender bias is intended by this wrting style.

Acknowledgments

I would like to thank my fellow breeders of the NSCA for their support in supplying contributions of text, photos, and ideas. I would also like to thank my family, Brent, Brody, Colby, Haylee, JD, John, Juilianna, Kelsie, and Preston for their unflagging support and encouragement throughout this project.

All inquiries should be addressed to:
Barron's Educational Series, Inc.
250 Wireless Boulevard
Hauppauge, NY 11788
www.barronseduc.com

ISBN: 978-0-7641-4743-2
Library of Congress Catalog Card No. 2012023522

Library of Congress Cataloging-in-Publication Data
Payton, Laura.
Shiba inus : everything about selection, care, nutrition, behavior, and training / Laura Payton.—2nd ed.
p. cm.—(Pet owner's manual)
Includes index.
ISBN 978-0-7641-4743-2
1. Shiba dog. I. Title.
SF429.S63P38 2012
636.76—dc23   2012023522

Printed in China
9 8 7 6 5 4 3 2 1